Talking About Rakugo
The Stories Behind the Storytellers

KRISTINE OHKUBO
With Kanariya Eiraku

Copyright © 2022 by Kristine Ohkubo.

All rights reserved. No part of this publication may be reproduced, distributed or transmitted in any form or by any means, including photocopying, recording, or other electronic or mechanical methods, without the prior written permission of the author, except in the case of brief quotations embodied in critical reviews and certain other noncommercial uses permitted by copyright law. For permission requests, contact the author using the website address provided below.

https://kristineohkubo.wixsite.com/nonfiction-author

Talking About Rakugo 2/Kristine Ohkubo. —1st ed.

ISBN 978-1-0879-8459-9

Since early 2020, the COVID-19 pandemic has been spreading across the globe with alarming speed and creating many hardships. On August 27, 2021, rakugo storyteller Sanyutei Takasuke passed away after being infected with the new coronavirus. He was 54. At the time of writing this book, there were over 5 million COVID-19 related deaths worldwide.

During these unsettling times, and despite the many dangers, performers have stepped forward to entertain us and allow us momentary escapes from the harsh reality of living through this pandemic.

I dedicate this book to those individuals who, through their art, strive to create a better, more enjoyable world for us.

ACKNOWLEDGEMENTS

I would like to express my sincere gratitude to those who purchased the first rakugo book, *Talking About RAKUGO — The Japanese Art of Storytelling*, and openly encouraged me to write a second book as a follow-up. Your favorable reviews and comments galvanized me to delve deeper into the world of rakugo and share my discoveries with you.

I hope you will relish this journey with me.

"One of the main reasons that rakugo became popular is that it became diversified.

There are many types of storytellers now.

Diversity of the rakugoka has contributed to a positive outcome."

– Shunputei Shota, rakugo storyteller

TABLE OF CONTENTS

Introduction x

Meet the Characters 1

   1. Tachibanaya Bunzo III 3
   2. Hayashiya Kosome IV 8
   3. Yanagiya Koman III 13
   4. Kawayanagi Senryu 19
   5. Tatekawa Rakucho 26
   6. Sanyutei Kyuto 33

Nisei (Second Generation) Performers 41

   7. Hayashiya Shozo IX 43
   8. Hayashiya Sanpei II 47
   9. Yanagiya Karoku 52
   10. Sanyutei Oraku 59
   11. Hayashiya Kikuzo II 64
   12. Katsura Yonedanji V 70
   13. Katsura Ryoba 74
   14. Katsura Shuncho III 79

The Contemporary Superstars 83

   15. Tatekawa Shinosuke 85
   16. Shunputei Shota 92
   17. Yanagiya Kyotaro 97
   18. Katsura Bunshi VI 103

The Interviews...109

   19. Katsura Fukuryu 111

   20. Katsura Utazo 126

   21. Stéphane Ferrandez 132

   22. Kanariya Koraku 147

   23. Kanariya Simon 157

   24. Kanariya Usagi 168

The Scripts..179

   Big Sale (*Oh-Yasuuri*) 182

   Bloodline Stamp (*Okechimyaku*) 194

   Complimenting a Child (*Kohome*) 201

   Hamlet (*Hamuretto*) 210

   The Matsuyama Mirror (*Matsuyama Kagami*) 220

   Shiba Beach (*Shibahama*) 228

   Short Life (*Tanmei*) 246

   The Wallet (*Kami-ire*) 256

List of Photos and Illustrations 266

Works Cited 268

About Us 278

i. Gonsuke's Lantern (*By Kei Ohsuga*)

Translation:

Master: *"I'll go home."*

Gonsuke: *"You are disliked by both of them."*

INTRODUCTION

Approximately 400 years ago, long before modern comedians developed the onstage presentation style recognized as stand-up comedy, a distinct form of comedic storytelling began to emerge in Japan. The art form developed primarily in urban areas such as Edo (Tokyo), Kyoto, and Osaka, and evolved into two distinct performance styles: Edo and Kamigata (Osaka). It became known as *rakugo* during the middle of the Meiji period (1868–1912), and it remains an integral form of live entertainment today.

Utilizing a feudalistic apprentice system, this minimalistic art of storytelling was verbally passed down from one generation to the next from master to disciple. The traditions that were established all those years ago continue to be practiced today, but adherence to the old and tried has not prevented rakugo from evolving during the modern age. Today, the stage once dominated by Japanese raconteurs has expanded to include a number of foreign practitioners. Additionally, rakugo is no longer presented in the Japanese language only. Rakugo performed in English and other languages such as French continues to gain popularity among audiences in Japan and overseas.

Rakugo storytelling is a unique performance that uses gestures and narration rather than costumes and props; and it requires a high degree of skill. A rakugo story is comprised of both narrative and dialog between multiple characters, all of which are conveyed by a single storyteller. The storyteller strives to express the personality of each character by differentiating their tone of voice, choice of words, manner of speaking, and other factors.

The realm of rakugo is inhabited by unique and congenial characters with which an average person can easily identify. Only in this domain will you encounter a complete but likeable fool like Yotaro, simpleton craftsmen like Hachigoro and Kumagoro, an adolescent apprentice like Sadakichi, and an irresponsible young master named Kotaro who spends all his time playing around in the pleasure quarter.

In principle, the only props permitted in rakugo are the *sensu* (a folding paper fan) and *tenugui* (a hand towel). These items are given a great deal of versatility in the stories as they are used to represent a wide range of items.

It is the job of the *rakugoka* (professional storyteller) to inspire their audience's imagination through their skills in portraying the realm and characters of each story. At the time of writing this book, there were approximately 1,000 professional storytellers in Japan, and countless amateur storytellers hailing from all walks of life. Each one brings his or her own experiences, eccentricities, and authenticity to the unique world of rakugo.

Sometimes, the stories behind the storytellers entice the public as much as the stories they tell on stage. Rakugo storytellers are often as unique and interesting as the various characters they portray.

Meet the Characters

ii. Tachibanaya Bunzo III (*Photo by Kanariya Eiraku*)

1. TACHIBANAYA BUNZO III

"I remember being told by my master that rakugo is a business that manipulates words, so use proper Japanese."
— *Tachibanaya Bunzo III* [1]

Tokyoite Tachibanaya Bunzo stepped into the world of rakugo in October 1986 at the age of 24. He chose to study with master Tachibanaya Bunzo II (1939-2001) because he aspired to learn rakugo from someone who was faithful to the basics. He was promoted to *futatsume* (second level storyteller) in 1990 and elevated to *shinuchi* (master storyteller) status in September 2001. But Bunzo's joy was overshadowed by the sorrow of losing his beloved master that same month.

Fifteen years later, Bunzo inherited his master's stage name and became the third generation Tachibanaya Bunzo. During the press conference to announce his succession, Bunzo humbly stated, "I am honored to be able to inherit the name of my master. I want to spread the name of Tachibanaya Bunzo all across Japan."[2]

---

[1] "「ちゃんとした日本語を使いなさい」．橘家文蔵が語る「師匠に教わった大切なこと」．" 文春オンライン. 文藝春秋, September 19, 2020. https://bunshun.jp/articles/-/40369?page=1.
[2] サンスポ "橘家文左衛門、襲名披露会見で宣言「文蔵の名前を広めていきたい」." サンスポ. サンスポ, August 29, 2021. https://www.sanspo.com/article/20160907-5E5E62AXOBMV3PKQJNHRZPKIZ4/.

Bunzo (previously known as Bunzaemon) was a regular on the BS Nippon Television series, *BS Shoten* (later renamed *Shoten Jr.*), a sister program to the highly popular weekly television show *Shoten*. *Shoten* first aired on May 15, 1966, and it is currently the second-longest running television variety show in Japan. *BS Shoten's* announcer often jokingly introduced Bunzo to the audience as "the model prisoner in the dressing room."[3]

Indeed, Bunzo is a dynamic character with an impressive brawny appearance and a gruff voice. He injects these characteristics into his rakugo performances, but he is careful not to alter the basic structure of the stories themselves. Whether he is portraying Inkyo (the old man), Hachigoro, or Kumagoro, all of the rakugo characters he depicts are offshoots of his own personality. This makes his rakugo truly unique and one of a kind.

One of the stories Bunzo truly enjoys performing is called "*Rakuda*" ("Camel"), about a gang member who is disliked by everyone. Rakugo includes many stories that were adapted from kabuki plays, but "Rakuda" is one of the few rakugo stories adapted into a kabuki play. As the story unfolds, Rakuda passes away from *fugu* (puffer fish) poisoning, and his fellow gang member, Hanji, has to find a way to conduct a funeral service for him. Bunzo's portrayal of the gang members in the story is so

---

[3] "橘家文蔵 (3代目)." Wikipedia. Wikimedia Foundation, July 3, 2021. https://ja.wikipedia.org/wiki/%E6%A9%98%E5%AE%B6%E6%96%87%E8%94%B5_(3%E4%BB%A3%E7%9B%AE).

convincingly realistic that it actually frightens people. During one performance, fellow rakugoka Kokontei Shincho was in the audience. After watching Bunzo's performance, Shincho said, "It was good but a bit scary."[4]

Several years ago, Bunzo offered a rakugo class specifically for amateur performers. He regularly gathered at a bar with his students after that day's lessons were over. On one such occasion, one of his students, Hanpeiji, approached him and told him that he was having trouble acting out a part in a story called "*Gojo-kyu*" ("Stubborn Moxibustion").

The story involves moxa, an herb harvested from the mugwort plant, which is commonly used in Chinese medicine. One of the characters in the story has to endure the pain of burning moxa placed on his skin. The student confessed that he did not know how to act this part out as he had never experienced the sensation of burning moxa on his skin. Bunzo, who was drinking alcohol and smoking a cigar at the time, placed his lit cigar on his pupil's arm. The young man yelled out in pain, and Bunzo calmly said, "Like this."[5]

In 2020, with the COVID-19 pandemic surging, Bunzo was one of the first rakugo storytellers to offer performances online. His shows, *Bunzo Gumi* (Bunzo Group) *Rakugo*, featured his long-time

---

[4] Kanariya, Eiraku. TACHIBANAYA BUNZO III (3代目橘家文蔵), May 21, 2021.
[5] Kanariya, Eiraku. TACHIBANAYA BUNZO III.

friend Yanagiya Kyotaro, Shunputei Ichinosuke, Kokontei Kikunojo, Tatekawa Danshun, and Yanagiya Kosen. The performances, which were filmed without an audience, were first made available only to the Bunzo Gumi fan club members and were free of charge. But eventually, they were opened up to include the general paying public when the risk of coronavirus infections prevented people from enjoying live rakugo performances in the theaters.[6]

In addition to performing rakugo, Bunzo also engages in live music presentations. He is one-third of a musical trio named *San K Shinbunsha*. The band features Bunzo and fellow rakugoka Yanagiya Kosen and Irifunetei Sentatsu. The band derives its name from the names of the three performers, "tatsu" (which can also be pronounced "shin" in kanji form) from Irifunetei Sentatsu, "bun" from Bunzaemon, Bunzo's former stage name, and "sha" from Reireisha Wakaba, Kosen's former stage name.

The group focuses on Showa period (1926–1989) music and features songs by popular Japanese musicians such as Sada Masashi, Izumiya Shigeru, and Sawada Kenji. Bunzo plays the guitar and percussion instruments, Sentatsu plays the guitar and

---

[6] "【オンライン配信】4/22（水）19:30〜第3回文蔵組落語会 ゲスト：立川談春師匠." 三代目 橘家文蔵 Official Website (Third Generation Bunzou Tachibanaya Official Website). Accessed August 30, 2021. https://www.bunzou.com/116240.html.

the piano, and Kosen plays the guitar and the *shinobue* (Japanese transverse flute).⁷

---

⁷ 産経ニュース "【鑑賞眼】三Ｋ辰文舎落語＆ライブ 噺家たちの二刀流 昭和のにおいがするラインアップ (Sankei News)." 産経ニュース. 産経ニュース, April 16, 2016. https://www.sankei.com/article/20160417-QQO4746Y6ZIYHO7YOK43APJBPM/.

2. HAYASHIYA KOSOME IV

In a certain clan, two drunken samurai quarrel. One of them slashes and kills the other, and then he also dies.

After learning about the incident, the lord prohibits anyone from drinking alcohol. A guard station is set up at the gate of the mansion, and even the items brought in by merchants who come and go are inspected.

— Synopsis of "Kinshu Sekisho" ("No Liquor Checkpoint") performed by Hayashiya Kosome IV [8]

Although he spent only a fleeting moment among us, Osaka native Hayashiya Kosome still managed to leave his mark on the world of Kamigata rakugo.

Kosome lost his father when he was only eight years old, and he decided to become an apprentice of rakugo master Hayashiya Somemaru when he was just a junior high school student. After being rejected by Somemaru he continued on to high school, where he joined a rakugo study group with fellow classmate Shofukutei Tsuruko. The two boys belonged to the same drama club, and when Tsuruko created a rakugo study group, he and Kosome were

---

[8] "禁酒番屋." Wikipedia. Wikimedia Foundation, May 28, 2021.
https://ja.wikipedia.org/wiki/%E7%A6%81%E9%85%92%E7%95%AA%E5%B1%8B.

its only members. They took turns performing rakugo for each other. Later, Tsuruko wrote in his book, "I enjoyed being able to openly discuss rakugo with someone. I became more interested in rakugo after meeting Kosome. The more we talked, the more I grew to value rakugo."[9]

During his first year in high school, Kosome once again attempted to become Somemaru's apprentice. One day, he recited a rakugo story for Somemaru. At its conclusion, the master responded, "It isn't very funny, but I can sense your passion."[10] Kosome dropped out of high school and officially became Somemaru's *uchi-deshi* (live-in apprentice) on January 10, 1964. He tried to convince his friend Tsuruko to become Somemaru's student as well, but Tsuruko refused. He went to study with Shofukutei Shokaku VI after graduating from high school.

In June 1968, master Somemaru passed away from pancreatic cancer. On the evening of his funeral, Kosome declared that he did not want to join the Katsura or the Shofukutei houses of rakugo. He decided to focus his efforts on cultivating the Hayashiya group with Hayashiya Someji II (later Hayashiya Somemaru IV) instead.

Four years later, Kosome joined a group of young rakugo storytellers called The Panda. The group consisted of Kosome,

---

[9] "林家小染 (4代目)." Wikipedia. Wikimedia Foundation, August 22, 2020. https://ja.wikipedia.org/wiki/%E6%9E%97%E5%AE%B6%E5%B0%8F%E6%9F%93_(4%E4%BB%A3%E7%9B%AE).
[10] " 林家小染 (4代目)." Wikipedia.

Tsukitei Happo, Katsura Kinshi, and Katsura Bunchin. The foursome first got together on the MBS Television program *Young, Oh! Oh!* Kosome's subsequent television appearances helped boost his popularity and he soon became a household name in Japan.

But eventually the offers to appear on television began to dry up, and he again directed his attention to rakugo. He began giving solo performances with greater frequency and dreamed of succeeding to his master's stage name. After seeing his performances and witnessing his dedication to his art, rakugo master Shofukutei Shokaku VI wrote to him and told him, "If you continue to devote yourself like this, the name Hayashiya Somemaru will no longer be only a dream."[11]

Unfortunately, Kosome never actually realized his dream. He was a heavy drinker and often found himself in unfortunate circumstances due to his drunkenness. In an inebriated state, he cursed master Shokaku, frequently climbed utility poles, and at one point used a closet to relieve himself. He never denied that he was an alcoholic and stated, "I'm sure alcohol will kill me some day."[12]

Kosome's premonition came true on January 29, 1984. After drinking heavily at a restaurant in Minoh City, he wandered drunk

---

[11] 林家小染 (4代目)." Wikipedia.
[12] Toracchi. "『四代目林家小染』." とらっちのアホちゃいまんねんパーデンネンブログ. Ameba, July 21, 2020. https://ameblo.jp/toratchi-1021/entry-12612578412.html.

onto National Highway Number 171. A car hit Kosome and he sustained a severe head injury, which left him unconscious. The accident was immediately reported by every television station in Osaka. The reports mentioned that Kosome was involved in a traffic accident and had been taken to a nearby hospital. He never regained consciousness and died two days after the accident, at the age of 36.[13]

During his funeral on February 7, Hayashiya Someji mourned and said, "How happy I would be if these flowers were being used to celebrate your succession to the name of Hayashiya Somemaru IV instead."[14]

---

[13] Toracchi. "『四代目林家小染』 (4th Hayashiya Kozome)."
[14] "林家小染 (4代目)." Wikipedia.

iii. Yanagiya Koman III (*Photo by Yomuiri Newspaper/Aflo Images*)

3. YANAGIYA KOMAN III

"Rakugo became popular during the Edo period because people were bored. There wasn't any fighting for over 260 years."

— *Yanagiya Koman III* [15]

In a world where the performers convey their stories verbally and rely on spontaneity to keep their art fresh and alive, rakugoka Yanagiya Koman is known for preparing scripts prior to taking the stage and later selling them on the Internet. Koman, who has transcribed over 350 stories, follows in the footsteps of his first master, Katsura Bunraku VIII.

Bunraku habitually jotted down his stories before taking the stage. He painstakingly captured every element and even placed marks on where to breathe during the storytelling process. Like his master, Koman is also dedicated to capturing his stories exactly as he performs them on stage. If he happens to deviate from the written script while on stage, he will go back and make adjustments to the script to reflect those changes. When he initially began to transcribe his stories by hand, the scripts became messy and illegible as he made change after change. He later discovered

---

[15] "Special Lecture: Master Yanagiya Koman III (Rakugoka)." JSA Institute, October 2018. www.jsa-net.or.jp.

the word processor, which made making changes much easier. Today, rather than rely on a computer, he has four word processing machines he depends on to record his large catalogue of rakugo stories.[16]

Koman dropped out of the Tokyo University of Agriculture and Technology at the age of 19 to pursue rakugo under the tutelage of master Bunraku.[17] He was given the *zenza* (apprentice rakugoka) stage name of Katsura Koyu as an homage to Bunraku's favorite Japanese tanka poet and playwright, Isamu Yoshii. The kanji characters for the name "Isamu" can also be read as "yu;" therefore, Bunraku combined the poet's first name with the word "*ko*" ("small") to create a stage name for his disciple. He attained the level of futatsume in March 1965, but he lost his master before he was qualified to be promoted to shinuchi.

Following Bunraku's death in 1971, Koman went to study with master Yanagiya Kosan V, the first rakugoka to be recognized as a Living National Treasure in Japan. Four years later, at the age of 33, he finally became a shinuchi.

Koman's performance style clearly demonstrates that he is the product of both masters. He displays both Bunraku's refinement

---

[16] "落語家が話芸を活字で残す理由 柳家小満ん師匠すでに２７巻をネット通販." 産経ニュース" (Sankei News). 産経ニュース, January 26, 2018.
https://www.sankei.com/article/20180128-TSP745L7EBM2FIZ4DZFKGFS5EY/.
[17] "柳家小満ん." Wikipedia. Wikimedia Foundation, July 28, 2021.
https://ja.wikipedia.org/wiki/%E6%9F%B3%E5%AE%B6%E5%B0%8F%E6%BA%80%E3%82%93.

and Kosan's comedic style when he takes the stage. He is also a rakugoka who composes haiku poems and produces various essays. He has contributed numerous essays to the monthly rakugo magazine *Tokyo Kawaraban*.[18] The essays which were initially published under the heading, "*Hanashi no Hosomichi wo Aruku*" ("Walking Along Narrow Paths to Stories"), were later compiled in a book titled *Edo Tokyo Rakugo Sanpo* (2009).[19]

Forty years after becoming a master storyteller, Koman began publishing his rakugo stories in booklet form, which he calls *Tekisuto* (*Text*). The booklets are self-produced using a word processor and sold to the general public by mail order.[20] The production and sales of the bi-monthly publication are handled by the members of Tekisuto no kai. The group was originally founded to assist with the reception and other matters related to Koman's monthly small-scale rakugo performances, which only lasted for a period of two years.

In addition to being inspired by his master's rituals, a previously published collection of rakugo scripts in shorthand also motivated Koman to capture his own stories in writing. The stories in this book were transcribed in shorthand as they were being performed on stage. Over the years, the book has served as a valuable

---

[18] Radio Cafe, Inc. "アーティストプロフィール (Artist Profile/Yanagiya Koman)." 柳家小満ん | アーティストプロフィール | ラジオデイズ. Accessed September 5, 2021. https://www.radiodays.jp/artist/show/180.
[19] Kanariya, Eiraku. YANAGIYA KOMAN III (3代目柳家小満ん), September 6, 2021.
[20] "柳家小満ん." Wikipedia.

reference guide for Koman. He publishes *Tekisuto* with the hope that it too will serve as a reference guide for others. The vast majority of those who purchase *Tekisuto* are other rakugo storytellers.

Although his first master, Bunraku, only performed 30 carefully selected stories in his lifetime, Koman has a much larger repertoire to draw from. Even with the recurrent publication of *Tekisuto*, he still has approximately 200 unpublished stories in his arsenal.[21] Among his extensive collection of tales is a story he created, "*Achitari Kochitari*" ("Here and There"), about a drunken man who invents endless excuses to tell his wife for not coming home on time.[22]

Koman performs the same story only once every ten years, and he has committed a substantial number of stories to memory.[23] He began his solo performances, called Koyu no kai, in 1969. After his promotion to shinuchi, he changed the event's name to Koman no kai to reflect his new stage name. These shows still take place at the Oedo Nihonbashitei theater in Tokyo's Chuo City during each odd-numbered month. As of March 2020, which marks the beginning of the outbreak of the COVID-19 pandemic, Koman has given 300 solo performances at this venue.

---

[21] "落語家が話芸を活字で残す理由 柳家小満ん師匠すでに２７巻をネット通販."
[22] Kanariya, Eiraku. YANAGIYA KOMAN III (3代目柳家小満ん).
[23] "落語家が話芸を活字で残す理由 柳家小満ん師匠すでに２７巻をネット通販."

In 1994, he added another series of solo performances, this time in his hometown of Yokohama. The Yokohama Yanagiya Koman no kai ended a quarter century later with a total of 150 performances given.[24]

Now in his later years, Koman continues to actively learn and perform new stories. He is driven by the words of his master, Bunraku, who said, "The one who studies wins."[25]

---

[24] Kanariya, Eiraku. YANAGIYA KOMAN III (3代目柳家小満ん).
[25] "落語家が話芸を活字で残す理由 柳家小満ん師匠すでに２７巻をネット通販."

iv. Kawayanagi Senryu (*Photo by Mainichi Newspapers/Aflo Images*)

4. KAWAYANAGI SENRYU

"Bushido is no good. It disrespects human life."

— Kawayanagi Senryu

(An aside during the performance of "Gakon.") [26]

Kawayanagi Senryu is a storyteller who has made a name for himself by performing rakugo that is completely divorced from the long-established traditions of the art form. At age 15, Senryu left Saitama Prefecture and journeyed to Tokyo at his father's urging. There, he pursued various odd jobs, and by 1951, he was living and working at a liquor store, where he acquired a strong taste for alcohol. As a result, he has been prone to frequent bouts of drunkenness over the years.

Senryu turned his attention to rakugo in 1955 and began studying under the guidance of master Sanyutei Ensho VI. He was given the stage name of Sansho, where "san" means "three" and "sho," which incorporates the last part of his master's name, means "living." Although Ensho agreed to take him on as his second apprentice, their master-apprentice relationship was always a little strained. This was because Sansho did not represent Ensho's ideal image of a rakugoka; and he preferred *shinsaku rakugo* (new

---

[26] "夏と終戦とガーコンと(Natsu to Shūsen to Gākon to)." 夏と終戦とガーコンと｜【西日本新聞me】. 西日本新聞me, August 19, 2018. https://www.nishinippon.co.jp/item/n/442336.amp.

original rakugo stories) over the time-honored *koten rakugo* (classical stories) his master favored.

To make matters worse, Sansho's frequent drunkenness resulted in an unfortunate incident at his master's house just two years after being accepted as an apprentice. Sansho visited Ensho's home in an inebriated state and defecated in the *genkan* (entranceway). Although the incident continues to be a blemish on his career, it did not prevent him from being promoted to futatsume in September 1958.

In 1959, Sansho received an invitation to join the Toho Company's *rakugo benkyo-kai* (rakugo study group), but he was later dismissed for being involved in a ruckus. In 1965, he was selected as a member of *Shoten*. However, after filming of the first episode, he managed to anger the show's host, Tatekawa Danshi, and was kicked off the program.

In September 1974, with the intervention of rakugo master Sanyutei Enraku V, ten rakugo performers were promoted to shinuchi as a group. Ensho, who was a champion of koten rakugo, objected to Sansho's promotion on the basis that he only performed shinsaku rakugo and interlaced his stories with jazz. In protest, he did not participate in any of the official events associated with the group's promotion.

Then in May 1978, the death knell finally tolled for Sansho. When Ensho withdrew from the *Rakugo Kyokai* (Rakugo Association) with his disciples and formed the *Rakugo Sanyu Kyokai* (Rakugo Sanyu Association), Sansho initially told his master that he would join him. Later that evening after he returned home, he had a change of heart and decided to remain with the Rakugo Kyokai. That decision resulted in his excommunication. On May 28, 1978, Ensho telephoned Sansho and asked that he relinquish his stage name. On the same day, Sansho met with Hayashiya Shozo VIII and Yanagiya Kosan V. Kosan agreed to take him as a disciple and renamed him Kawayanagi Senryu.

Senryu accepted his first and only disciple in March 1997.[27] Kawayanagi *Tsukushi* (named for a wild plant known as Japanese horsetail) was 28 years old at the time. She was a graduate of Waseda University, and she had studied under Kaname Okitsu, a scholar of early modern literature who specializes in comic storytelling. Her studies provided her with ample opportunities to visit the *yose* (a vaudeville-type theater where rakugo is performed), after which she resolved to pursue professional rakugo upon graduating.[28] Her stage name was given to her by Senryu's wife. Tsukushi was promoted to shinuchi in September 2014 — and she is only the fourth female to attain that level as a member of the Rakugo Kyokai.[29]

Following in her master's footsteps, Tsukushi composed her own shinsaku rakugo story, *"Ensho e no Michi"* ("The Road to Ensho").

---

[27] "川柳川柳." Wikipedia. Wikimedia Foundation, July 27, 2021.
https://ja.wikipedia.org/wiki/%E5%B7%9D%E6%9F%B3%E5%B7%9D%E6%9F%B3.
[28] "川柳つくし." Wikipedia. Wikimedia Foundation, January 28, 2021.
https://ja.wikipedia.org/wiki/%E5%B7%9D%E6%9F%B3%E3%81%A4%E3%81%8F%E3%81%97.
[29] "川柳川柳." Wikipedia.

The premise of the tale is determining who will succeed to the stage name of Ensho, a prominent name on the rakugo world's family tree. In the story, after considerable debate, her master Senryu is chosen to succeed.[30]

Among Senryu's many shinsaku rakugo stories, the most popular one is called "Gakon." The story derives its title from the sound made by the foot pedal of a rice threshing machine. The narrative, which incorporates military songs and jazz, is considered to be Senryu's masterpiece.[31] Other rakugoka such as Kokontei Ucho, Tachibanaya Bunzo, and Yanagiya Kosen have also performed this story on stage. Senryu himself has delivered this tale to audiences more than 100 times a year. At one point, he even performed "Gakon" in tandem with Kosen.[32]

Senryu also incorporated music into other shinsaku rakugo stories such as "*Jazz Musuko*" ("Jazz Son") and "La Malagueña." "Jazz Musuko" is a story about the post-war youth of Japan who fell in love with jazz music. A father who loves *Gidayu-bushi*, the traditional music heard in a puppet theater, complains about his son who loves jazz music.[33] One day, the father begins playing Gidayu-bushi on the first floor while his son and his friends

---

[30] Kanariya, Eiraku. KAWAYANAGI SENRYU (川柳川柳), September 7, 2021.
[31] "川柳川柳." Wikipedia.
[32] Kanariya, Eiraku. KAWAYANAGI SENRYU.
[33] "Gidayu-Bushi: Music of the Japanese Puppet Theatre." prezi.com. Accessed September 7, 2021. https://prezi.com/rkg_i7vpbmg_/gidayu-bushi-music-of-the-japanese-puppet-theatre/#:~:text=What%20is%20it%3F,the%20audience%20and%20evoking%20emotion.

simultaneously play jazz on the second floor. Senryu stopped performing this story in 2011 at the age of 80 because it required a lot of energy to enact.[34]

He began performing "La Malagueña" during his futatsume years, which helped his popularity soar, much to the chagrin of his master Ensho. The song "La Malagueña" (also known as "Malagueña Salerosa") is a well-known Huapango song from Mexico. The lyrics are about a man telling a woman (from Málaga, Spain) how beautiful she is and how he would love to be her man, but that he understands her rejecting him for being too poor.[35] Senryu defies the conventions of rakugo by singing the song during his act, playing his guitar, wearing a sombrero, and telling short erotic stories.[36]

In addition to his musical rakugo, Senryu has produced several rakugo stories which are considered non-broadcastable. In fact, there was a well-known incident while he was still Ensho's apprentice. He was scheduled to perform at the Toho Meijinkai which had a strict rule about what types of stories could be performed. Senryu performed a story which contained the word *omanko* (referring to a woman's private part) and was severely reprimanded by his master. Later, Ensho, who also delivered such

---

[34] Kanariya, Eiraku. KAWAYANAGI SENRYU.
[35] "Malagueña Salerosa." Wikipedia. Wikimedia Foundation, July 30, 2021. https://en.wikipedia.org/wiki/Malague%C3%B1a_Salerosa.
[36] Kanariya, Eiraku. KAWAYANAGI SENRYU.

stories from time to time, reflected on the incident and said he was not qualified to scold his disciple.[37]

The rakugo world lost Kawayanagi Senryu on November 17, 2021. He was 90 years old. He summarized his unconventional life in a memoir he released in 2009 titled, *Yose bakushō-ō gākon rakugo ichidai*. In an article contributed to the Mainichi newspaper following his death, Masakazu Yui wrote, "He turned the pain during and after the war into art, loved sake and songs, and took his own path. It was a remarkable 90-year life."[38]

---

[37] "川柳川柳." Wikipedia.
[38] Yui, Masakazu. "落語家・川柳川柳さん死去　90歳　「ガーコン」で異彩放つ (Rakugoka Senryu Kawayanagi Dies 90 Years Old)." 毎日新聞. 毎日新聞, November 19, 2021. https://mainichi.jp/articles/20211119/k00/00m/040/104000c.

v. Tatekawa Rakucho (*Photo by Yomiuri Newspaper/Aflo Images*)

5. TATEKAWA RAKUCHO

"Laughter prevents the three leading causes of death in Japan."

– Tatekawa Rakucho
Shizuoka Shimbun (September 24, 2012)

Rakugo attracts people from all walks of life, and Tatekawa Rakucho is a very good example. A disciple of Tatekawa Shiraku, he was a practicing physician before officially stepping into the world of rakugo. Born in Iida City, Nagano Prefecture in 1954, he began working at the Keio University School of Medicine shortly after graduating from medical school. He belonged to a rakugo study group while at university, and he continued to engage in rakugo after leaving school.

Tatekawa Rakucho entered the world of professional rakugo in April 1998 as a guest disciple of Tatekawa Shiraku. Two years later, at the ripe age of 46, he officially became Shiraku's apprentice and lived a dual life as a rakugo storyteller and a doctor. During the *Tatekawa-ryu* (the Tatekawa school) New Year's party on January 2, 2004, he managed to impress Shiraku's master and the school's founder, Tatekawa Danshi, with his storytelling and was promoted to futatsume in April that same year. He attained shinuchi status in October 2015.[39]

Combining his training as a physician and a rakugoka, he developed a new genre of rakugo known as health rakugo, a mixture of rakugo and health education.[40] Rakucho aspired to spread health education through laughter and released 13 CDs and eight books related to health rakugo. His last book, *Waratte ikireba, warratte shineru* (*If You Live Laughing, You Can Die Laughing*) was published in February 2021, just three months before his death.

Rakucho's health rakugo included original stories about cancer, smoking, dementia, and diabetes, among other health-related topics. One of the stories, "Gokon Rojin-kai," is about a government sponsored *gokon* (group blind date) for senior citizens. The event proves to be such a huge success that some of the elderly attendees begin dating each other regularly. A few even become entangled in a love triangle. In true rakugo fashion, in the end, their dementia vastly improves.[41]

Growing up in Nagano, Rakucho did not have a lot of exposure to rakugo storytelling. It wasn't until he became a junior high school student that he began watching rakugo on television and was

---

[39] "立川らく朝." Wikipedia. Wikimedia Foundation, May 14, 2021. https://ja.wikipedia.org/wiki/%E7%AB%8B%E5%B7%9D%E3%82%89%E3%81%8F%E6%9C%9D.
[40] オフィスらく朝. "プロフィール: 健康落語の立川らく朝." プロフィール | 健康落語の立川らく朝. Accessed September 6, 2021. https://rakuchou.jp/profile/index.html.
[41] Kanariya, Eiraku. TATEKAWA RAKUCHO (立川らく朝), September 8, 2021.

spellbound by its charm. It was also around this time that he saw master storyteller Tatekawa Danshi on television for the first time.

After junior high, he left rural Nagano behind to attend high school in Tokyo, where he became involved in numerous extra-curricular activities. He joined the drama club, the literary club, and the art club. On weekends, he went to the Shinjuku Suehirotei yose theater to watch rakugo.[42]

Rakucho's acting ambitions accompanied him to the Kyorin University School of Medicine. There, he entertained the idea of putting on a play, but he could not gather enough student actors to stage it. Instead, he organized a rakugo study group and, as its only member, performed rakugo for the student body. Eventually, he began to focus more on rakugo and less on theatrical acting. In his junior year in medical school, he founded the Federation of Rakugo for Medical Students in Kanto.[43]

Once he began working as a physician; however, he gradually tapered his rakugo activities. He became so busy that he had no time left to focus on storytelling. On occasions, when he got drunk, he began asking himself, "Why am I not doing rakugo?"[44]

In December 1996, he joined a rakugo study group called Rakujuku, which was presided over by Tatekawa Shiraku. It was

---
[42] オフィスらく朝. "プロフィール: 健康落語の立川らく朝."
[43] Kanariya, Eiraku. TATEKAWA RAKUCHO (立川らく朝).
[44] オフィスらく朝. "プロフィール: 健康落語の立川らく朝."

a monthly gathering of rakugo lovers who listened to Shiraku's rakugo theory and learned practical rakugo skills. Rakujuku rekindled Rakucho's passion for rakugo. Approximately one year after joining the study group, his desire to perform rakugo professionally began to grow stronger. Finally, in March 1998, he decided to request a formal introduction to master Shiraku.

Even though Rakucho requested an introduction, he could not lay aside his trepidation that as a middle-aged man with a wife and children, he would be out of place among Shiraku's younger disciples. Despite his initial uncertainty, he decided to push forward.[45] Naturally, Shiraku refused to accept him as a disciple because Rakucho was ten years older, but he had a change of heart after seeing how enthusiastic he was.[46]

Rather than accepting him as a regular apprentice, Shiraku offered him the opportunity to learn rakugo as a guest disciple. Being a guest disciple is literally unheard of in rakugo, but Rakucho appreciated his master's kindness and willingness to teach him rakugo this way. He was obligated to pay a monthly fee for the lessons, which in a sense made his rakugo training seem more like a private lesson than an actual apprenticeship.

Rakucho hung around the performance venues and dressing rooms for almost two years, and he managed to learn over 50

---

[45] オフィスらく朝. "プロフィール: 健康落語の立川らく朝."
[46] Kanariya, Eiraku. TATEKAWA RAKUCHO (立川らく朝).

stories as a guest disciple.⁴⁷ He decided to approach his master once again and asked about becoming a real zenza. Shiraku was at a loss about what to do and consulted his master, Danshi, who advised him to accept Rakucho as an apprentice.⁴⁸

Following the death of Tatekawa Danshi, the Tatekawa-ryu instituted a system by which a futatsume would be promoted to a shinuchi. The eligible candidates were required to give six rakugo performances and ask the audience to vote on who they believed was the most suitable for the promotion. The candidate with the highest number of total votes was unconditionally promoted to the shinuchi level. The promotions of those that were left behind would then fall into the hands of the Tatekawa-ryu Board of Directors.

Rakucho's first promotion performance was held in October 2014. The final performance came six months later on April 4, 2015. He managed to win the overall number of votes and was promoted to master storyteller. His official promotion took place on October 1, 2015.⁴⁹

Rakucho was able to perform rakugo as a master rakugoka for a little over five years. Ironically, the doctor who pioneered health rakugo died from illness on May 2, 2021, at the age of 67. After

---

⁴⁷ オフィスらく朝. "プロフィール: 健康落語の立川らく朝."
⁴⁸ Kanariya, Eiraku. TATEKAWA RAKUCHO (立川らく朝).
⁴⁹ オフィスらく朝. "プロフィール: 健康落語の立川らく朝."

learning about his death, his master Shiraku bemoaned, "Why did you go before your master?" He added, "You will be a grand master in the afterworld."[50]

In a strange twist of fate, Rakucho had examined Shiraku and discovered that he had Basedow's disease (also known as Grave's disease). The disorder causes hyperthyroidism; excess thyroid hormones are produced and could lead to a thyroid storm, resulting in a rapid heartbeat, fever, fainting, and even death. After his diagnosis, Shiraku exclaimed, "You became my disciple in order to save my life!"[51]

---

[50] Sanspo.com. "立川らく朝さんの訃報に志らく「師匠より先に逝くやつがあるか」." SANSPO.COM. サンケイスポーツ, May 11, 2021. https://www.sanspo.com/smp/geino/news/20210511/geo21051123230023-s.html.
[51] Kanariya, Eiraku. TATEKAWA RAKUCHO (立川らく朝).

vi. Sanyutei Kyuto (*Photo by Yomiuri Newspaper/Aflo Images*)

6. SANYUTEI KYUTO

"It's like strawberry daifuku. It's a surprising combination at first, but once you try it, it's delicious."

— *Sanyutei Kyuto, regarding musical rakugo (2017)*

If Tatekawa Rakucho was known for his health rakugo, Sanyutei *Kyuto* (Cute) is known for his musical rakugo. Known as Sanyutei Arou until 2014, this singing rakugoka once called himself "Evita," based on the musical by Andrew Lloyd Webber.

In 1988, Kyuto joined the *Gekidan Shiki* (Shiki Theatre Company), one of Japan's best-known and largest theatre companies. Growing up, he admired Bruce Lee and Matsuda Yusaku, a Japanese actor best known for his roles in action films. When he reached high school age, he worked up the courage to tell his parents that he wanted to become an actor, but they responded with anger to his career choice. Kyuto had no alternative but to take the university entrance examination and enroll in a vocational school in Tokyo.

After his 21st birthday, he registered at an actor training school in Tokyo, but he was soon forced to return home to Kagawa. There, he joined an amateur theater company while he helped his father with the family's construction business. Kyuto was torn between his desire to pursue acting and his obligation to help with his family's business. Then one day, he visited a fortune-teller in Kurashiki who advised him to join the Shiki Theater Company.

Kyuto was already 25 years old when he became a member of Gekidan Shiki. The founder of the theater company, Asari Keita, encouraged him by telling him, "Look at your own watch. Each person has his or her own time. Don't rush."[52] Deciding to follow his own pace, he remained a member for ten years and performed in musicals and stage plays such as "Hamlet," "Evita," and "Jesus Christ Superstar" both at home and overseas.

In his thirties, Kyuto once again found himself at the crossroads. He had seen a rakugo performance on television and fell in love with the art form. He always wanted to pursue realism as an actor and he recognized that rakugo would offer him an opportunity to realize his ambition. He was impressed with a storyteller's ability to realistically portray certain acts such as eating soba noodles and drinking alcohol on stage. He thought that one person having the chance and ability to portray multiple characters alone was wonderful in itself. He wanted to try his hand in rakugo. But he was already 34 years old and earning a decent salary; he didn't know what to do. He visited a fortune-teller once again and said, "I'm a stage actor, but I want to be a rakugo storyteller."[53] The fortune-teller advised him to pursue rakugo.

---

[52] "劇団四季から落語家に…三遊亭究斗「ミュージカル落語」で伝えたいこと."
[53] " 劇団四季から落語家に…三遊亭究斗「ミュージカル落語」で伝えたいこと."

Reassured, Kyuto set about finding a rakugo master to teach him. Scanning through a magazine, he learned that Shunputei Koasa, Yanagiya Kosanji, and Kokontei Shincho all had solo performances scheduled in Kyushu. But only Koasa's performance did not conflict with Kyuto's theatrical commitments.

After seeing Koasa's performance, Kyuto became determined to learn rakugo from him. He wrote a letter to the master and gave it to a manager during a performance in Saga the next day. Koasa read the letter and came out to see Kyuto. He said, "Aren't you wasting your time? The life of a rakugoka is a difficult one." Kyuto responded heartily and said, "I really want to do it!"[54]

In 1997, he became the apprentice of Shunputei Koasa, who was eight years his senior and also an actor.[55] After three years of training, Kyuto became very impatient. He wanted to advance to the rakugo stage quickly. Then came a period when Koasa excommunicated one disciple after another. There was a rumor circulating that Kyuto would be excommunicated also.

At that time, another master rakugo storyteller, Sanyutei Enjo, said, "If he is excommunicated, I will take over."[56] Enjo was open to accepting Kyuto because he himself had been responsible for

---

[54] "劇団四季から落語家に…三遊亭究斗「ミュージカル落語」で伝えたいこと."
[55] "三遊亭究斗." Wikipedia. Wikimedia Foundation, June 28, 2021. https://ja.wikipedia.org/wiki/%E4%B8%89%E9%81%8A%E4%BA%AD%E7%A9%B6%E6%96%97.
[56] "劇団四季から落語家に…三遊亭究斗「ミュージカル落語」で伝えたいこと."

popularizing shinsaku rakugo stories in Tokyo. Throughout his career, Enjo had produced 300 shinsaku rakugo stories. In 2001, Kyuto officially became the disciple of Sanyutei Enjo and was promoted to futatsume in 2002. From that point on, he continually straddled the worlds of professional rakugo and musical theater.

In 2003, he auditioned for and won the part of Thénardier in the vastly popular "Les Miserables," a musical adaptation of Victor Hugo's 1862 novel. Beginning in 2005, and lasting for a period of three years, he made regular appearances on the television theater program *Opera ch* and served as its host.

Since 2004, he has been creating his own original musical rakugo, a fusion of rakugo and musical theater, and attracting the attention of non-traditional rakugo fans. His long list of original stories includes "The Misora Hibari Story," which is based on a famous Japanese singer and actress whose career spanned 42 years, "The Elvis Presley Story," *The Sound of Music*, *West Side Story*, and "The Louis Armstrong Story (Jazz Rakugo)." Kyuto also adapted a story from the popular stage musical, *Miss Saigon*. His version is called "*Miss Saikon*" ("Miss Remarriage").[57]

Kyuto is versatile and also likes to perform koten rakugo stories such as "*Bunshichi Mottoi*" ("Bunshichi's Hairband Shop"), a story created by the legendary rakugoka Sanyutei Encho (1839-1900).

---

[57] Eiraku, Kanariya. Anecdotes: Kyuto, August 19, 2021.

Adapted from a tale originating in China, the story is considered difficult to perform because it is so long and has many characters to portray.[58]

The story begins with a skilled plasterer named Chobei who doesn't work and gambles all day. As a result, he has a lot of debts, and one day he even loses the clothes off his back. Deprived of everything, he arrives home to learn that his daughter, Ohisa, is missing. Later, he is notified by a messenger from a brothel he frequents that his daughter plans to sell her body to pay down her father's debts. Chobei rushes over to the brothel where the madam, Okado, gives him 50 *ryo* (the currency unit of the Edo period) with the condition that he must return it by the last day of the year or Ohisa will be forced to work in the brothel.

On his way home, Chobei encounters a servant named Bunshichi who is contemplating suicide. When he asks the man why he is planning to kill himself, he learns that the man was sent to collect money and had been pickpocketed. He plans to kill himself to make up for the loss. To save him, Chobei gives Bunshichi the 50 ryo he received from the madam.

Bunshichi returns to his master and presents him with the 50 ryo given to him by Chobei. The master incredulously asks where he

---

[58] "三遊亭究斗." Wikipedia. Wikimedia Foundation, June 28, 2021.
https://ja.wikipedia.org/wiki/%E4%B8%89%E9%81%8A%E4%BA%AD%E7%A9%B6%E6%96%97.

obtained the money and shows him another 50 ryo which was returned to him after Bunshichi had left it behind while being engrossed in a board game called Igo. Shocked, Bunshichi confesses the entire story.

The next day, Chobei is in the *nagaya* (row house) where he lives and a visitor arrives, telling Chobei what transpired. The visitor offers to return the 50 ryo Chobei had given to Bunshichi, but he refuses to accept it by stating that once an Edo citizen gives something to someone, he cannot take it back.

Eventually, Chobei is talked into accepting the money. Ohisa returns home after her mother pays the madam the money she loaned to Chobei. Later, Bunshichi and Ohisa marry and open a hair band shop together.[59]

The story is a classic *ninjobanashi* (tragicomic human-interest story), and it is included with Kyuto's 30 original musical rakugo stories in his repertoire.

In 2014, Kyuto finally attained the top level of shinuchi along with Yanagiya Tozaburo, Yanagiya Sangoro, Kokontei Shinko, and Katsura Yamato.

---

[59] Yu, A. C. "Bunshichis Mottoi - Japanese Wiki Corpus." Bunshichis Mottoi - Japanese Wiki Corpus. Accessed September 9, 2021. https://www.japanese-wiki-corpus.org/culture/Bunshichis%20Mottoi.html.

He is also an officially certified child psychology counselor. He released a book in 2020 titled *To You Who Are Bullied*. Kyuto, who had been bullied himself as a child, describes his history in the book and begs readers to "think seriously about bullying."[60]

---

[60] "三遊亭究斗." Wikipedia.

Nisei (Second Generation) Performers

vii. Hayashiya Shozo IX (*Photo by Nippon News / Alamy Stock Photo*)

7. HAYASHIYA SHOZO IX

"When I was a kid, I was picked on because I was Sanpei's son. I said my dad should quit his job where he is laughed at. Then mom got angry and said we are making a living because he is laughed at. After that I stopped complaining about my father's job."

— *Hayashiya Shozo IX* [61]

Rakugoka and television personality Hayashiya Shozo is a person who has rakugo coursing through his veins. He is the eldest son of Hayashiya Sanpei I, who was a vastly popular and dominant force in the worlds of rakugo and television during the Showa era. His grandfather was rakugoka Hayashiya Shozo VII. His younger brother is Hayashiya Sanpei II, a regular on the television program *Shoten*.

Following in his father's footsteps, who had apprenticed under his own father before becoming the disciple of Tachibanaya Enzo VII, Shozo became the apprentice of Sanpei I at the age of 16. It was originally thought that he would be given the stage name of Kosanpei, but instead he came to be called Kobuhei (derived from the Japanese word *kobuta* and meaning piglet). This was because

---

[61] "林家正蔵 (9代目)." Wikipedia. Wikimedia Foundation, August 12, 2021.
https://ja.wikipedia.org/wiki/%E6%9E%97%E5%AE%B6%E6%AD%A3%E8%94%B5_(9%E4%BB%A3%E7%9B%AE).

his younger brother had quipped, "Because my brother is fat, I think Kobuhei is a good name for him."[62] Shozo was obviously unhappy with the stage name given to him by his father and later recalled, "My father was not good at naming his disciples."[63]

After his father passed away in 1980, Shozo became a disciple of his father's apprentice, Hayashiya Konpei. He was promoted to shinuchi on March 21, 2005 and adopted his current stage name at that time. That same year, it was revealed that his master was suffering from multiple sclerosis, a neurological disease that causes body paralysis. This impacted both his ability to perform on stage and to train his apprentices. Konpei passed away on December 21, 2020, at the age of 77.

Having worked as a child actor in the 1970s, Shozo also appears on various dramas and variety shows in addition to performing rakugo. In 1990, he provided the voice on the anime *Oishinbo* for a character named Kissho Senkichi; like Shozo, he is a second generation rakugoka.[64]

In the story, Kissho's father, Fukufukutei Suekichi, sends him to study under Kairakutei Hassho. Kissho progresses well and advances to shinuchi, after which he proposes to Hassho's daughter and also asks permission to succeed to the name of

---

[62] " 林家正蔵 (9代目)." Wikipedia. Wikimedia Foundation, August 12, 2021.
[63] "林家正蔵 (9代目)." Wikipedia.
[64] "林家正蔵 (9代目)." Wikipedia.

Fukufukutei Suekichi II. His master refuses both requests and Kissho storms out, but he is unable to work as a rakugoka.

One day, he is invited to perform rakugo at a restaurant and is unaware that his former master will be in the audience. Following his successful performance, his master declares that as long as Kissho remains as humble as the meals served at this particular restaurant, he will become the second generation Suekichi.[65]

In addition to his rakugo storytelling and acting jobs, Shozo began working as a visiting professor at Josai International University in 2005. In 2008, he published a book called *Chishiki zero kara no jazu nyumon* (*Introduction to Jazz from Zero Knowledge*).

Shozo is a great lover of jazz music and he maintains a collection of over 10,000 records and CDs. He occasionally appears on radio programs as a jazz critic and has contributed articles to the Japanese Jazz magazine *Swing Journal* under his real name, Ebina Yasutaka.[66]

---

[65] "List of Oishinbo Episodes." Wikipedia. Wikimedia Foundation, August 18, 2021. https://en.wikipedia.org/wiki/List_of_Oishinbo_episodes.
[66] "林家正蔵 (9代目)." Wikipedia.

viii. Hayashiya Sanpei II (*Photo by Nippon News / Alamy Stock Photo*)

8. HAYASHIYA SANPEI II

"The vibrant New Year's scene changed completely after my father's death. The people who gathered together each year disappeared like a tide.

I know my mother sometimes went into my deceased father's study alone and cried softly."

— *Hayashiya Sanpei II, from his book,*
Chichi no Senaka — Sessha no Hansei *(2009)*

When Sanpei I passed away, his younger son was only nine years old at the time. Unlike his older brother, Hayashiya Shozo IX, Sanpei II did not get the opportunity to learn rakugo from their father. Instead, he entered the world of rakugo in 1990 as an apprentice to their father's disciple and Shozo's second master, Hayashiya Konpei. He was given the stage name of Hayashiya Ippei and did not have to suffer the humiliation his older brother had with his first stage name, Hayashiya Kobuhei.

Sanpei had enrolled at Chuo University in the Department of International Economics in 1989, but he dropped out to study rakugo full-time. He attained the level of futatsume in 1993, and he was promoted to shinuchi in 2002. In May 2009, he succeeded to his father's stage name and became the second generation Hayashiya Sanpei. His older brother, Shozo, declined to inherit their father's stage name because he wanted he and his brother to perpetuate their grandfather's and father's names in the world of rakugo.

Although he primarily performs rakugo in Japanese, Sanpei has delivered rakugo performances in other languages while traveling outside Japan. In 1999, he performed the story *"Kinshu Banya"* ("The Prohibition") in English while visiting Singapore. In 2006, he visited China and performed *"Dobutsuen"* ("The Zoo") in Chinese. He returned to China the following year and delivered the story *"Okiku no Sara"* ("Okiku's Dishes") in Chinese. Unlike his father, Sanpei is more of a traditionalist and favors koten rakugo stories. When he participated in the Daiginza Rakugo Festival in 2005, he chose to perform the popular classical rakugo story *"Tokisoba"* ("Time Noodles").[67]

The first generation Hayashiya Sanpei, was known as the "Showa King of Laughter," and made countless television, film, and radio appearances during his career in addition to performing as a rakugoka. Sanpei II also engages in numerous activities as a television personality.[68] He met his future wife, actress Kokubu Sachiko, on the Japanese historical drama *Mito Komon*, the longest-running period drama in Japanese television history. Sanpei

---

[67] "林家 三平 | 一般社団法人 落語協会." 一般社団法人 落語協会. Accessed August 26, 2021. https://rakugo-kyokai.jp/variety-entertainer/member_detail.php?uid=151.
[68] "林家三平 (2代目)." Wikipedia. Wikimedia Foundation, August 9, 2021. https://ja.wikipedia.org/wiki/%E6%9E%97%E5%AE%B6%E4%B8%89%E5%B9%B3_(2%E4%BB%A3%E7%9B%AE).

appeared on the program for six episodes in 2010 and 2011. Sachiko only appeared on two episodes in 2009 and 2011.[69]

On May 29, 2016, Sanpei made his first appearance on Nippon Television's *Shoten*, wearing a beige kimono and blending into the background among those who sit on stage with their sky-blue, pink, yellow, purple, and orange kimonos. Before joining the show as a regular, he made a guest appearance on the 40th anniversary special, which featured rakugo masters and their disciples. The program was broadcast on May 14, 2006.[70]

In 2005, Sanpei along with other second generation rakugoka from the Tokyo and Kamigata families formed a rakugo group known as Bochan 5 (Greenhorn 5). The group consisting of Sanpei, Sanyutei Oraku, Hayashiya Kikuzo II, Katsura Shuncho, and Tsukitei Hakko got together for the Daiginza Rakugo Festival held at the Ginza Komatsu Hall on July 17, 2005. The group stages various rakugo performances together and are known to get along well with one another both in private and in public.

Sanpei also oversees the *Negishi Sanpei-do* (Negishi Sanpei Museum), a memorial museum established in honor of his father. The museum was established 15 years after his death and exhibits

---

[69] "Mito Kômon." IMDb. IMDb.com, August 4, 2010.
https://www.imdb.com/title/tt1172114/.
[70] "林家三平 (2代目)." Wikipedia.

various belongings and memorabilia. The Negishi Sanpei-do also hosts several rakugo performances throughout the year.

On his Rakugo Kyokai (Rakugo Association) profile, Sanpei states, "I want to be a rakugoka who will be loved by people."[71]

---

[71] "林家 三平 | 一般社団法人 落語協会."

ix. Yanagiya Karoku (*Photo by Yomiuri Newspaper/Aflo Images*)

9. YANAGIYA KAROKU

"At the autograph session after I performed the koten rakugo story 'Shibahama,' I wrote, 'I did Hamamatsu.'"

— Yanagiya Karoku, discussing his struggles with dyslexia, Mainichi Shimbun (2021)

Yanagiya Karoku is a second-generation rakugoka with quite an impressive pedigree. His maternal grandfather was Yanagiya Kosan V, the first rakugo storyteller to be designated as a Living National Treasure. His uncle is Yanagiya Kosan VI; his brother is former ballet dancer and choreographer Kobayashi Juichi; his father is actor, artist, and singer Wada Keishu; and his mother is former actress Kobayashi Kimiko.

With DNA like that, it is hard to believe that Karoku would grow up to be anything but a rakugo storyteller. Even though Kosan and Karoku were related, a formal introduction is always required in the world of rakugo. Karoku was formally introduced to his rakugo master by his mother at the age of 15. Kosan was 72 years old at the time and Karoku was the last disciple he trained.[72]

---

[72] "柳家花緑." Wikipedia. Wikimedia Foundation, August 8, 2021. https://ja.wikipedia.org/wiki/%E6%9F%B3%E5%AE%B6%E8%8A%B1%E7%B7%91.

Karoku displayed a brilliance for the art of rakugo early in life and attained shinuchi status when he was only 22, becoming the youngest master rakugoka at the time. As he began to accept apprentices, he questioned whether he was qualified to do so at such a young age. He approached his rakugo master, who offered him these words of wisdom, "Take on disciples because to teach is to learn."[73] Inspired by his master's insight, Karoku continued to accept apprentices.

He also quickly shifted to television and appeared on several well-known programs including NHK Educational TV's language variety show *Nihongo de Asobo* (*Play with Nihongo*). He became popular among children after performing the story "Jugemu" on the show in 2006.[74]

One of rakugo's most famous stories, "Jugemu" centers around a couple who could not think of a suitable name for their newborn baby boy, so the father went to the temple and asked the priest to think of an auspicious name. The priest suggested several names, beginning with Jugemu. The father could not decide which name he preferred and gave the baby all of the names. So, Jugemu's full name is Jugemu, Jugemu, Goko-no Surikire, Kaijarisuigyo-no, Suigyomatsu Unraimatsu Furaimatsu, Kuunerutokoro-ni Sumutokoro, Yaburakoji-no Burakoji, Paipopaipo Paipo-no

---

[73] Ohkubo, Kristine, and Kanariya Eiraku. Talking about Rakugo: The Japanese Art of Storytelling, 42-43. Los Angeles, CA, 2021.
[74] "柳家花緑." Wikipedia.

Shuringan, Shuringan-no Gurindai, Gurindai-no Ponpokopi-no Ponpokona-no, Chokyumei-no Chosuke.

In one version of the tale, Jugemu gets into a fight with a friend one day, and the friend sustains a large bump on his head. In protest, he goes crying to Jugemu's parents. However, due to the amount of time it took to recite his name, by the time he finished saying it the bump on his head had already healed.[75]

In an effort to popularize rakugo, Karoku participates in a wide range of activities, mainly among the younger age groups.[76] In his endeavors to take modern rakugo to the next stage, he has experimented with performing rakugo wearing a suit and sitting in a chair. When rakugo first became popular during the Edo period (1603 to 1867), the storyteller and the audience were both dressed in kimono and sat on *zabuton* (floor cushions). In time, the audience adopted modern clothing, but the rakugoka continued to wear kimono. As a result, the commonality that was once shared by the storyteller and the audience was replaced by a detachment between them.

Karoku wants to change the perception of rakugo as a traditional art and align it more with other forms of modern entertainment. He also feels that kimono and floor cushions are an impediment to

---

[75] "Jugemu." Wikipedia. Wikimedia Foundation, September 9, 2021. https://en.wikipedia.org/wiki/Jugemu.
[76] "柳家花緑." Wikipedia.

the globalization of rakugo. He maintains that these are the things of which rakugo must divest itself in order to be accepted by foreign audiences.[77]

He believes that since rakugo stories appeal to the audience's imagination, it really does not matter what the storyteller is wearing. Karoku selected a suit to replace the kimono on stage because the kimono is regarded as Japanese formal wear. Certainly, rakugo can also be performed in a T-shirt and jeans, but you will almost never see a rakugoka performing in a casual *yukata* (cotton summer kimono).

When it comes to producing original shinsaku rakugo stories, Karoku makes his own adaptations, but he relies on teaming with other talented writers to produce stories from scratch. In 2010, he collaborated with screenwriter and playwright Mashiba Azuki to produce a story based on Miyabe Mizuki's book, *Our Neighbors' Crimes*. The story is similar to the koten rakugo tale, "*Sangen Nagaya*," where people living in the middle of a row house conspire to get rid of their noisy neighbors.[78]

---

[77] Shinozaki, Hiroshi. "New Innovation 'Suit Rakugo' Karoku Yanagiya Tries New Work with a Chair." 朝日新聞デジタル：朝日新聞社のニュースサイト. Asahi Digital, December 22, 2008. http://www.asahi.com/showbiz/stage/rakugo/TKY200812220175.html.

[78] "新たなるスタイルで落語に新風を吹き込む柳家花緑に その手法や舞台で披露する'新作落語'について、そして巨星・立川談志への思いを聞いた！- インタビュー＆レポート: ぴあ関西版." 新たなるスタイルで落語に新風を吹き込む柳家花緑に その手法や舞台で披露する"新作落語"について、そして巨星・立川談志への思いを聞いた！- インタビュー＆レポート | ぴあ関西版WEB, January 18, 2012. http://kansai.pia.co.jp/interview/stage/2012-01/120118-e006.html.

Despite all of his efforts to modernize rakugo and increase its appeal to younger generations, Karoku still has a certain attachment to the past. He appeared in a series of commercials for the Japanese tombstone company known as Sudo Sekizai Co., a company which his grandfather had helped promote when he was alive.[79]

These days, Karoku holds his grandfather's teachings dear to his heart. While Kosan was alive, Karoku found that he had to maintain a certain distance between them in order for their master-disciple relationship to work. His grandfather's words naturally became more precious after he was gone.[80]

In 2001, Karoku became engaged to a female rakugoka, Hayashiya Kikuhime, a disciple of rakugo master Hayashiya Kikuo. The couple were to get married in 2002, but the wedding was postponed after Kosan passed away on May 16, 2002. The couple separated in May 2009, and on April 10, 2010, Karoku married a woman four years his senior.

Karoku revealed in 2017 that he had been struggling with a learning disability, dyslexia, all his life. He detailed his experiences in a book he released in April 2020 called *Boku ga Teni Ireta Hattatsu Shogai to iu Tomarigi* (*A Perch Called a Developmental Disorder That I*

---

[79] "柳家花緑." Wikipedia
[80] "新たなるスタイルで落語に新風を吹き込む柳家花緑に その手法や舞台で披露する'新作落語'について、 そして巨星・立川談志への思いを聞いた！"

Gained). As of the writing of this book, he has authored 16 books and co-authored/contributed to nine others.[81]

---

[81] "柳家花緑." Wikipedia.

x. Sanyutei Oraku (*Photo by Yomiuri Newspaper/Aflo Images*)

10. SANYUTEI ORAKU

"I'm standing on the edge of despair. I'm not the least bit interested in succeeding to my father's name."

— Sanyutei Oraku, commenting on his disappointment after not being able to succeed to his master Enraku's stage name (2009)[82]

Rakugo storyteller Sanyutei Koraku, a regular on the television show *Shoten*, shares a special relationship with his son, Sanyutei Oraku. Both father and son were apprentices of Sanyutei Enraku V, a prominent rakugo master and a member of a group of extraordinary rakugo performers known as the *Edo Rakugo Wakate Shitenno* (Edo Rakugo's Four Young Heavenly Kings). In fact, Oraku was Enraku's 27th and last disciple. He was introduced to Enraku in May 2001 and received his promotion to futatsume three years later. After Enraku retired on February 25, 2007, he said in an interview, "I think I have to do my best until Oraku becomes a full-fledged rakugoka." Enraku was in rather poor health at the time, and his comment was his affirmation to hang on long enough to fully train his last disciple.[83]

---

[82] "三遊亭王楽." Wikipedia. Wikimedia Foundation, May 19, 2021.
https://ja.wikipedia.org/wiki/%E4%B8%89%E9%81%8A%E4%BA%AD%E7%8E%8B%E6%A5%BD.
[83] "三遊亭王楽." Wikipedia.

Oraku's father began his rakugo training with master Hayashiya Hikoroku in 1966. After Hikoroku passed away in January 1982, Koraku continued his training with master Enraku. Oraku's real name, Kazuo, was given to him by Hikoroku.[84] His rakugo stage name comes from the nickname his master was given when he was young, *Hoshi no Ohji-sama* (The Little Prince). Oraku was derived from the "Oh" in *Ohji-sama* (Prince) and "raku" taken from his master's stage name, Enraku. At times, he called himself The Little Prince II, but he never managed to achieve the popularity his master did.[85]

As Enraku's disciple, Oraku dreamed of inheriting his master's name upon being promoted to shinuchi, but he lost that privilege to Enraku's senior disciple, Sanyutei Rakutaro. Rakutaro succeeded to their master's stage name and became Sanyutei Enraku VI in 2010. After learning the news, Oraku said, "I'm standing on the edge of despair. I'm not the least bit interested in succeeding to my father's name." Oraku became a shinuchi in October 2009.[86]

In 2005, he joined a rakugo group known as Bochan 5. The group, which consists of other second generation rakugoka, was formed for the 2005 Daiginza Rakugo Festival. Members Oraku and

---

[84] "三遊亭王楽." Wikipedia.
[85] Kanariya, Eiraku. SANYUTEI ORAKU (三遊亭王楽), August 26, 2021.
[86] "三遊亭王楽 ." Wikipedia.

Kikuzo are both second generation rakugoka and their fathers are members of *Shoten*.

Oraku has mastered 100 stories, many of which he has only performed once. He prefers to focus on koten rakugo, but he has also incorporated original shinsaku stories such as Katsura Bunshi's "*Dokusho no Jikan*" ("Reading Time ") into his repertoire.[87]

This highly entertaining story opens with a man searching for a particular book on his bookshelf. The book is a pornographic novel disguised under a book cover belonging to another novel, *Ryoma ga Yuku* (*Ryoma Goes His Way*) written by renowned author Shiba Ryotaro. Sakamoto Ryoma was a samurai who led the Meiji Restoration. Unbeknownst to the man, his son happened to take the book to school for his class reading lesson.

During the reading lesson, the boy was asked to read a passage from the book aloud. He began reading, "Maya put her nails on Ryohei's back..." "Wait a minute! Isn't it Ryoma? Who is Ryohei?" The teacher realized that the book was different from what the book cover revealed and stopped him from reading further. She politely asked him to read from a different book.

---

[87] "三遊亭王楽." Wikipedia.

After learning what had happened, the man apologized to his son. Later, his son brought another book, this one about the Meiji Restoration, but it too turned out to be pornographic novel.[88]

Like other contemporary rakugo storytellers, Oraku has made numerous television appearances over the years on such programs as *Asaichi*, a Japanese weekday morning talk show airing on NHK Television, *Shoten*, and *BS Shoten*. He is an avid motion picture enthusiast and watches an average of 100 movies a year.[89]

---

[88] "読書の時間." Wikipedia. Wikimedia Foundation, June 28, 2015.
https://ja.wikipedia.org/wiki/%E8%AA%AD%E6%9B%B8%E3%81%AE%E6%99%82%E9%96%93.
[89] "Sanyutei Oraku Official Web Site." sanyuteiouraku.com. Accessed September 12, 2021.
https://www.sanyuteiouraku.com/profile.html.

xi. Hayashiya Kikuzo II (*Photo by Yomiuri Newspaper/Aflo Images*)

11. HAYASHIYA KIKUZO II

"A rakugoka does not have a retirement age."

— Hayashiya Kikuzo II, NHK Radio's Takeuchi Toko's Gogo Café
(June 25, 2021)

When the time came for Kikuzo to enter the world of rakugo, he followed the standard path of most father and son storytellers and became his father's disciple. His current stage name once belonged to his father, but it was given to him when he was promoted to shinuchi in September 2007.[90] While it is unprecedented for a rakugo storyteller to inherit his master's stage name while the master is still alive, Hayashiya Kikuzo I, who was battling stomach cancer in 2000, had stated that he wanted to live to see his son promoted to shinuchi and gift him with his stage name.[91] He also felt that his own fame would not guarantee his son's success; therefore, he wanted to bolster his entry into the world of rakugo by giving him an already well-recognized name.[92]

---

[90] "林家木久蔵 (2代目)." Wikipedia. Wikimedia Foundation, July 4, 2021. https://ja.wikipedia.org/wiki/%E6%9E%97%E5%AE%B6%E6%9C%A8%E4%B9%85%E8%94%B5_(2%E4%BB%A3%E7%9B%AE).
[91] "林家木久蔵 (2代目)." Wikipedia.
[92] "Special Issue Nippon Kichi/ Bakushō Rakugo-Ka No Kareinaru-Gei No Keishō." Accessed October 24, 2021. https://info.linkclub.or.jp/nl/2008_01_02/hayashiya.pdf.

Kikuzo was inspired by his father's performances on the television program *Shoten*, and he decided to become a rakugo storyteller.[93] Kikuzo I did not push his eldest son to become a rakugoka, and Kikuzo II later admitted that he probably would not have entered the world of rakugo if his father had pushed him.[94]

After graduating from the Department of Drama at Tamagawa University, he began studying rakugo with his father in 1996 and adopted the stage name of Hayashiya Kikuo. He was promoted to futatsume in 1999; however, when his father was diagnosed with cancer, he had to find someone else with whom to continue his rakugo training. That person was his father's close friend, Shunputei Koasa.[95]

Kikuzo I provided his son with a relaxed atmosphere in which to learn and taught him the basics of rakugo. Even so, Kikuzo II later confessed that as his father's disciple, he always had a sense that he was living and breathing rakugo every single minute of his existence. In an interview given to Nippon Kichi, he joked that within a 24-hour day, he was invested in rakugo for 23 hours and 30 minutes.

Once he was promoted to shinuchi, he became known as Hayashiya Kikuzo II, and at the same time, his father changed his

---

[93] "林家木久蔵 (2代目)." Wikipedia.
[94] "Special Issue Nippon Kichi/ Bakushō Rakugo-Ka No Kareinaru-Gei No Keishō."
[95] "林家木久蔵 (2代目)." Wikipedia.

own stage name to Hayashiya Kikuo (his son's former stage name). Even as a master storyteller, Kikuzo is still supported by his famous father. The two have given joint rakugo performances across Japan on many occasions and continue to appear together on stage.[96]

In May 2021, the 83-year-old Kikuo fell in his home and broke his left leg. As a result, he was hospitalized for three weeks. *Shoten*, which is filmed in advance, could only be broadcast through June 26 with Kikuo present. With Kikuo's recommendation, *Shoten's* host, Shunputei Shota, invited Kikuzo to sit in for his father on the program that was scheduled to be broadcast in July. Kikuzo, who was 45 at the time, promptly accepted the offer and appeared on the show wearing his father's familiar yellow kimono, which was too short for him and revealed his shins. With a shy grin, he introduced himself to the audience by saying, "I am a growing boy. I am Hayashiya Kikuzo II."[97]

Kikuzo is also adept at a traditional Japanese street art performed with a woven bamboo screen known as Nankin Tamasudare. The performance consists of a person manipulating a special screen made of loosely woven bamboo sticks while chanting a rhythmic

---

[96] "Special Issue Nippon Kichi/ Bakushō Rakugo-Ka No Kareinaru-Gei No Keishō."
[97] "骨折林家木久扇の代打、息子木久蔵が「笑点」出演 父おなじみの黄色い着物 - お笑い：日刊スポーツ." nikkansports.com. 日刊スポーツ, July 4, 2021.
https://www.nikkansports.com/entertainment/news/202107040000857.html.

poem. The performer uses the screen to portray the objects in the poem without stopping.

The screen is twisted and folded in many different ways to portray an object, and then it is brought back quickly to its original screen shape. Nankin Tamasudare is said to have been a popular form of entertainment that began in the Edo period. Today, it is performed out on the street, at parties, and even during rakugo performances as an *iromono* (variety act) in an attempt to make the shows more entertaining.[98]

xii. Nankin Tamasudare performance (*Photo courtesy of Kanariya Eiraku*)

---

[98] "Nankin Tamasudare." Wikipedia. Wikimedia Foundation, June 15, 2021. https://en.wikipedia.org/wiki/Nankin_Tamasudare.

Following in the footsteps of his famous father, Kikuzo has made appearances on several well-known television programs, including *BS Shoten*. On *BS Shoten*, he portrays a Yotaro-type character (the fool), similar to the character portrayed by his father on *Shoten*. He also travels and gives lectures on various subjects. His past presentations have included such topics as "Do Not Do Your Best to Raise Children," "Communication Techniques," and "Laughter Is the Best."[99]

Kikuzo was married on February 18, 2006, and his first child, a daughter, was born in November of the same year. His second child, a boy, was born two years later. He made his rakugo debut as Hayashiya Kota in May 2016, at the age of eight.[100]

---

[99] "Hayashiya Kikuzo Profile (Kouen Plus)." 講演会・セミナー・イベントの講師紹介はコーエンプラス. Accessed September 12, 2021. https://kouenplus.com/profile/hayashiya_kikuzo/.
[100] "林家木久蔵 (2代目)." Wikipedia.

xiii. Katsura Yonedanji V (*Photo by Ogiyoshisan*)

12. KATSURA YONEDANJI V

"I was born into a storyteller's family. I became a rakugo storyteller because I was the eldest son. I was given the name Kobeicho. It was an obvious name for the son of the great master, Katsura Beicho."

— Katsura Yonedanji V [101]

Born in Osaka's Minami Ward, Katsura Yonedanji is the son of rakugoka, Katsura Beicho III, only the second rakugo storyteller to ever earn the designation of Living National Treasure in Japan. Even so, when he told his famous father that he wanted to be a rakugo performer after high school, he was met with severe disapproval. Rather than expressing joy over his son's career choice, Beicho chided him by saying, "You are not good at talking and you are not funny." He further added, "When I was your age, I did not have the opportunity to go to college."[102] Although he was rejected and felt discouraged, Yonedanji still managed to perform rakugo with his two younger brothers during a high school festival.

---

[101] "桂米團治 (5代目)." Wikipedia. Wikimedia Foundation, August 1, 2021. https://ja.wikipedia.org/wiki/%E6%A1%82%E7%B1%B3%E5%9C%98%E6%B2%BB_(5%E4%BB%A3%E7%9B%AE).
[102] "桂米團治 (5代目)." Wikipedia.

He ultimately honored his father's wishes and enrolled at Kansei Gakuin University, but his hope of becoming a rakugoka was rekindled when his father's apprentice, Katsura Yoneji, commented, "It will be too late for him to become an apprentice after he graduates from the university."[103] Later, another disciple, Katsura Shijaku, said, "Let's make him a rakugoka," and Beicho agreed — with the condition that Yonedanji would only be taught one story. Beicho and Shijaku decided to give Yonedanji the stage name of *Kobeicho* (Little Beicho).

Yonedanji officially became Beicho's disciple in August 1978 while he was still in school. In October that same year, he gave his first performance at the Katsura Beicho Rakugo Kenkyukai. The performance was featured on NHK news, but Beicho still held firm that his son should finish school first. He reiterated his intent and told his son, "I couldn't go to school because of the war."[104]

Yonedanji continued his education and eventually graduated, but his rakugo training was not as successful. He had a poor memory, and as he was training with two of his father's other disciples who were good at memorizing, Yonedanji often got scolded.

Nonetheless, he gave several performances both alone and with his father or with his father's apprentices. He augmented his involvement with rakugo by becoming the accountant for the

---

[103] "桂米團治 (5代目)." Wikipedia.
[104] "桂米團治 (5代目)." Wikipedia.

Kamigata Rakugo Association. In 1992 he was awarded the Osaka Prefectural Theater Encouragement Award.

Yonedanji was good-looking and earned the nickname "the Nagashima Kazushige of the rakugo world." (Kazushige is the handsome son of legendary baseball player, Nagashima Shigeo. He is also an actor, a sports commentator, and a former professional baseball player.)

As Beicho's eldest son, Yonedanji had hoped to inherit his father's stage name, but those hopes did not materialize as stepping into the shoes of one of Japan's Living National Treasures is no easy task. Instead, in 2006, he made an attempt to succeed to the stage name of Tsukitei Kachou. That attempt failed and in the following year, Yonedanji announced at a press conference that he would take the stage name of Katsura Yonedanji V.

On March 19, 2015, Katsura Beicho died of pneumonia. Yonedanji was scheduled to perform the next day, and talked about his father's passing during his *makura* (prologue). The story he selected to perform was one of his father's favorite stories "*Jikoku Bakkei Moja no Tawamure*" ("The Ghosts Playing Around in Hell").

In the story, there is a scene where a ghost visits the yose theater. There is a sign posted at the entrance of the theater which reads, "Katsura Beicho coming soon!" This was one of the jokes Beicho cracked when telling the story. Yonedanji changed this part to

"Katsura Beicho coming today!" which he adapted as the ending punchline of the story on that particular day.

On June 22, 2016, Yonedanji was appointed the vice chairman of the Kamigata Rakugo Association. Two years later, he took over the Beicho Office Co. (a rakugo entertainment agency established by his father).[105] However, he resigned his position as president in March 2021, stating that he was both physically and emotionally unable to cope with the demands that were made on him.

In an interview he gave to the *Tokyo Kawaraban* magazine following his resignation, he said that the COVID-19 pandemic proved to be a game changer for him. Yonedanji had always been an "analogue" person, but he was forced to enter the digital world during the pandemic. He began by offering virtual rakugo performances and later redesigned the Beicho Office website to sell merchandise online.

When asked what his father would have said if he had still been alive, Yonedanji responded, "Just stay the way you are." That was Beicho's policy; he did not change regardless of the challenges he faced. When the Kobe Earthquake struck in 1995, Beicho was not rattled. He continued as before. Yonedanji said, "I want to be like him."[106]

---

[105] "桂米團治 (5代目)." Wikipedia.
[106] Kanariya, Eiraku. KATSURA YONEDANJI (桂米團治), August 25, 2021.

13. KATSURA RYOBA

"I had a great opportunity to hear rakugo at home. My dad was always practicing and I went to sleep listening to his tapes every night. But when I was a kid, I liked funny stories and stories that were easy to understand."

– Katsura Ryoba [107]

In the world of rakugo, it is not uncommon for the offspring of famous rakugo storytellers to pursue the art of storytelling themselves. Katsura Ryoba, a Kamigata rakugoka and a former drummer in the alternative rock band SHAME, is the eldest son of legendary rakugoka Katsura Shijaku II, dubbed the "King of Laughter." Although Ryoba ultimately entered the world of rakugo, he reached that point late in life and followed a long and winding path to get there.

When he was a child growing up in Toyonaka City, his life often revolved around rakugo. His father frequently took him to a *sento* (public bathhouse) on a bicycle after he finished practicing his rakugo in the afternoon, even though the family had their own bath at home. As a second grader, he went to sleep at night while

---

[107] Suda, Yasunari, and 須田 泰成「スローなコメディにしてくれ」編集長＋プロデューサー＋ライター。スローなコメディにしてくれ, 2017. http://www.slowcomedy.tv/978/2/.

listening to his father's rakugo records. If he woke up in the middle of the night, Shijaku put him back to sleep by reciting a rakugo story to him.

Ryoba became a member of the entertainment industry in 1990, when he became a member of a comedy troupe called Lilliput Army. In 1995, he formed the band SHAME with his younger brother, who goes by the name CUTT.[108] The band gained momentum performing at the Bahama music club in Osaka and produced a demo tape which reached Hide, who was then the lead guitarist for the Japanese rock band XJapan. Hide signed the group to his record label LEMONed, and they officially debuted in 1999 with their single, "Good-bye." Hide Matsumoto of XJapan passed away on May 2, 1998 in what was originally ruled to be a suicide, but later determined to be an accidental death. Ryoba's father, Shijaku, passed away from heart failure on April 19, 1999 after a failed suicide attempt.[109]

Ryoba retired from SHAME in 2008. Around this time, he began listening to his father's rakugo once again and was surprised by how much he enjoyed it.[110] Although he grew up with rakugo, he was selective and only enjoyed the stories that were interesting to

---

[108] "桂りょうば." Wikipedia. Wikimedia Foundation, June 15, 2021. https://ja.wikipedia.org/wiki/%E6%A1%82%E3%82%8A%E3%82%87%E3%81%86%E3%81%B0.
[109] rehow. "'Let's Meet Shame Now!" the Band Found in Hide (X Japan), the 20th Anniversary Live Vol.2 of Their Debut Will Be Distributed for Free on Youtube!" Japan NEWS, September 25, 2020. https://re-how.net/all/659724/.
[110] "桂りょうば." Wikipedia.

him as a child and easy to understand. As an adult, he found that he had an entirely different appreciation for the art form. He said in an interview given to Suda Yasunari in 2017, "I remember being able to laugh where I wasn't laughing in the old days, crying where I couldn't understand in the old days, and being shocked."[111]

In 2010, he participated in a rakugo study session with Tsukitei Hosei and began performing amateur rakugo under his real name, Maeda Kazutomo. In time, his passion for rakugo grew stronger.

The world of amateur rakugo provided the ideal environment for Ryoba to nurture his art. In fact, it was a rather encouraging atmosphere created by office workers, university professors, medical workers, fisherman, and farmers who went about their business during the day and gathered together at night to perform rakugo.[112]

On August 26, 2015, at the age of 43, he officially became the disciple of Katsura Zakoba II. In April 2017, he gave his first performance in Tokyo as Katsura Ryoba, a full-fledged rakugo storyteller.[113]

In April 2019, Ryoba premiered a program called "Ryoba's Rakugo Travel" on ABC Radio, in which he talked about rakugo with a

---

[111] Suda, Yasunari, and 須田 泰成「スローなコメディにしてくれ」編集長＋プロデューサー＋ライター。
[112] Suda, Yasunari, and 須田 泰成「スローなコメディにしてくれ」編集長＋プロデューサー＋ライター。
[113] "桂りょうば." Wikipedia.

guest. That same year, on the occasion of the 20th anniversary of their debut, SHAME reunited and released a new song called "Time Capsule." As their live concerts were greatly impacted by the pandemic, they streamed numerous performances live via the internet in 2020.[114]

---

[114] rehow. "'Let's meet Shame now!"

xiv. Katsura Shuncho III (*Photo by Yomiuri Newspaper/Aflo Images*)

14. KATSURA SHUNCHO III

"Empathy is the key to rakugo. Empathy has both yin and yang, and if laughter is yang, yin is tears. It's okay to have rakugo that conveys human stories, not just laughter."

– *Katsura Shuncho III* [115]

Not all offspring of rakugoka who ultimately follow the path to the rakugo world aspire to become storytellers as children. Katsura Shuncho, the son of rakugo storyteller, Katsura Shuncho II, wanted to become a nursery school teacher originally; however, following his father's death on January 4, 1993, he decided to pursue his parent's profession.

Soon after his graduation from high school in 1994, Shuncho apprenticed himself to his father's master, Katsura Harudanji III. He was first given the stage name of Haruna and succeeded to his father's stage name in August 2009. [116]

Concerned about how much influence Shuncho II had on his son, Harundanji sternly asked his new apprentice, "Will you be [taking] training as Shuncho's son, or will you begin learning

---

[115] "2017年2月25日（土）深夜1：45～2：40: ザ・ドキュメント: 関西テレビ放送 カンテレ." ザ・ドキュメント, 2017. https://www.ktv.jp/document/170225.html.
[116] "プロフィール: 桂春蝶 -かつらしゅんちょう- 公式サイト." 桂春蝶 -かつらしゅんちょう - 公式サイト | Just another WordPress site, January 10, 2020. https://shunchou.jp/profile/.

rakugo as my disciple?" Shuncho answered, "I would like to be your disciple."[117] Even so, he was not expected to succeed to his master's stage name after being promoted to shinuchi. When Harudanji passed away on January 9, 2016, Shuncho was the last disciple he trained. Another disciple, Katsura Harunosuke, succeeded to their master's stage name and became the fourth generation Katsura Harudanji in 2018.

Unlike the rakugo disciples of the past, most modern apprentices no longer live with their masters. After entering the world of rakugo at the age of 19, Shuncho lived in poverty for a period of about ten years, barely being able to afford the 29,000 yen (approximately $290) rent for his apartment. To make ends meet, he worked as a ski instructor at Hakuba Village in Nagano Prefecture during the day and performed rakugo for students at night. Although it was a miserable period in his life, he was grateful that he was able to work and save himself from starvation.

In 2005, he joined the rakugo group Bochan 5 with four other second-generation rakugo storytellers. In December 2011, he relocated from Osaka to Tokyo and divided his performances between the two cities. [118]

---

[117] "桂春蝶 (3代目)." Wikipedia. Wikimedia Foundation, August 10, 2021.
https://ja.wikipedia.org/wiki/%E6%A1%82%E6%98%A5%E8%9D%B6_(3%E4%BB%A3%E7%9B%AE).
[118] "桂春蝶 (3代目)." Wikipedia.

Like his father, he has produced a number of original shinsaku rakugo stories. While his father concentrated on humorous stories, such as "Pinocchio," Shuncho focuses on stories that are based on historical facts. In 2017, he created a story centered on the Battle of Okinawa. In order to ensure that his story was factual, Shuncho conducted extensive research and interviewed former nurses at the Army Hospital as well as Himeyuri students. The Himeyuri were a group of 222 students and 18 teachers at the Okinawa Daiichi Women's High School and Okinawa Shihan Women's School who formed a nursing unit for the Imperial Japanese Army during the Battle of Okinawa in 1945. Shuncho also talked with various women who cared for injured soldiers out on the battlefields.

His other original stories include "For You With A Future: The Story About Chiran Tokko," about a kamikaze suicide unit during the Second World War, and "To the Sea of Promise: The Story About the Distress of the Turkish Frigate Ertuğrul," about the shipwreck off the coast of Wakayama Prefecture in 1890.[119]

Shuncho selects human life as the underlying theme for most of his original stories, perhaps due in part to his father's early passing at the age of 51. Shuncho II was a heavy drinker and often gave up eating in favor of drinking sake instead. He was a frail man, who finally developed cirrhosis of the liver. Looking back on his

---

[119] Kanariya, Eiraku. KATSURA SHUNCHO III (桂春蝶), September 15, 2021.

father's non-stop drinking, Shuncho called it "a slow suicide."[120] When he performs his "human life" stories, Shuncho abandons the tradition of including a makura to warm up the audience before the story and launches into the tale immediately.

Over the years, as a member of the Kamigata Rakugo Association, he has organized the Hikohachi Rakugo Festival held at the Ikukunitama Shrine in Osaka. Yonezawa Hikohachi I, who died in 1714, is recognized as Osaka's pioneer professional storyteller. He is revered by modern rakugoka, who gather annually at the shrine where Hikohachi used to tell stories and pay homage to him. The two-day event features rakugo performances, street stands run by rakugo artists, amateur storytelling competitions, and much more.[121]

In August 2021, Shuncho tested positive for COVID-19 and was forced to postpone his rakugo show called *Kushikatsu no kai* ("Fried Skewered Cutlet Show"), in which he was scheduled to perform with Katsura Kaishi and Katsura Kichiya.[122]

---

[120] "2017年2月25日（土）深夜1：45〜2：40: ザ・ドキュメント: 関西テレビ放送 カンテレ." ザ・ドキュメント, 2017.
[121] "桂春蝶 (3代目)." Wikipedia.
[122] Kanariya, Eiraku. KATSURA SHUNCHO III (桂春蝶).

The Contemporary Superstars

xv. Tatekawa Shinosuke (*Photo by Yomiuri Newspaper/Aflo Images*)

15. TATEKAWA SHINOSUKE

"Take a simple example of the conversation between Hachi and Inkyo.

'Hello.'

'Oh, you're Hachi. Come on in.'

There are countless ways to place a pause in between these two lines. And each creates a different image. The pause is different every time we perform, and that's why we never get bored of performing rakugo."

— Tatekawa Shinosuke,
Tokyo Kawaraban (June 2020)

Today, a widely-recognized contemporary rakugo superstar, Tatekawa Shinosuke, did not have the privilege of growing up in the household of a well-known rakugo storyteller. Orphaned at a young age, he lived off the kindness and charity of his family members, which aided his resolve to become successful and independent.

Shinosuke's parents divorced when he was only four years old, and his mother passed away just one year later. He was forced to live with his maternal grandparents, who ran an antique shop in Shinminato City in Toyama Prefecture.

His grandfather was very fond of rakugo and introduced him to the art form at an early age. His family seldom missed watching Yanagiya Kosan V performing on television, but the young boy had no interest in rakugo at that point.

With financial assistance from his uncle, he entered the Faculty of Business Administration at the prestigious Meiji University. As a university student, he had a new-found interest in rakugo, joined the university *ochiken* (rakugo study group), and adopted the stage name of Shikontei Shiisho. But his pursuit of rakugo ended after graduation because he knew that he would not be allowed to work part-time while training as a rakugoka. After living off his uncle's charity for some time, Shinosuke wanted to be financially independent. He decided to study theater instead and work part-time.

While working part-time at a kushikatsu restaurant (a restaurant that serves deep-fried skewered meat and vegetables) and studying drama at the Subaru Theater Company, he met someone who was working for an advertising agency. This acquaintance recruited him for the Nitto Co. Ltd., an advertising agency in Kanazawa.

Soon after joining the agency, Shinosuke married a high school classmate. Then, at age 28, the president of the agency asked him about his future with the company. After thinking it over,

Shinosuke admitted that the time had come for him to leave the agency and pursue rakugo.

Although he had a strong admiration for Kokontei Shincho III while he was a university student, after seeing Tatekawa Danshi perform the story "*Shibahama*" ("Shiba Beach") at the National Engei Hall, he decided to pursue rakugo under Danshi's tutelage. Shinosuke was completely in awe of Danshi's delivery of "Shibahama," which was dramatically different from the conventional version of the story he was familiar with. In January 1983, at the age of 29, Shinosuke officially became an apprentice of Tatekawa Danshi and adopted his present stage name.[123]

That same year, two of Danshi's disciples, Tatekawa Danshiro and Tatekawa Kodanshi (now Kikutei Juraku IV) failed the shinuchi promotion test administered by the Rakugo Kyokai. But Hayashiya Genpei, a disciple of Hayashiya Sanpei who was believed to have been inferior to Danshi's apprentices, passed the examination. This angered Danshi, as he completely disagreed with the results and the criteria of the test. In protest, he left the Rakugo Kyokai with most of his apprentices and established the Tatekawa-ryu.[124]

---

[123] "立川志の輔." Wikipedia. Wikimedia Foundation, July 16, 2021.
[124] "落語立川流." Wikipedia. Wikimedia Foundation, October 5, 2021. https://ja.wikipedia.org/wiki/%E8%90%BD%E8%AA%9E%E7%AB%8B%E5%B7%9D%E6%B5%81.

Since he was no longer affiliated with the Rakugo Kyokai, which controlled the yose theaters in Tokyo, Shinosuke was unable to train and perform live during his zenza years. He had almost no income and was forced to accept work as a narrator from an acquaintance from his advertising agency days in order to earn a little money.[125]

All zenza have unique stories to share about their experiences with their masters, and Shinosuke is no exception, particularly since he was the disciple of the sometimes-eccentric Danshi. In the rakugo story *"Manju Kowai"* ("Scary Manju"), one of the characters brags that he can eat anything, even spiders. The character's lines typically go like this: "I also like spiders. I put their threads in *natto* (fermented soybeans) when the beans are not sticky enough."

One day, Danshi spotted a cobweb in the corner of the room near the ceiling and told Shinosuke to mix it with natto and eat it, to which his disciple responded, "Well, that's impossible *shisho* (master)."[126]

Shinosuke was promoted to futatsume and became independent in October 1984. In 1985, he accepted a job as a morning show reporter on TBS TV, and soon offers from various broadcasting

---

[125] "立川志の輔." Wikipedia. Wikimedia Foundation, July 16, 2021.
[126] Kanariya, Eiraku. Anecdotes: Shinosuke, August 19, 2021.

stations began to pour in. He also attained the level of shinuchi in May 1990.

Worried about the declining popularity of rakugo, he and five rakugo artists from Tokyo and Osaka founded the *Rokunin no Kai* (Group of Six) in March 2003. The group was the brainchild of Shunputei Koasa, a Tokyo rakugo storyteller, who is just a year younger than Shinosuke. Together they hosted various rakugo events, including the Daiginza Rakugo Festival from 2004 to 2008, and popularized rakugo among young Japanese people.

In February 2008, Shinosuke's original shinsaku rakugo story "*Kanki no Uta*" ("Ode to Joy") was made into a movie, and he was given a cameo role as a rakugo storyteller.[127] The story is based on the Japanese custom of chorus groups gathering to sing Beethoven's "Ode to Joy" on New Year's Eve.[128]

During the Ginza Rakugo Festival in 2007, Shinosuke, who almost always performs his rakugo in Japanese, presented the story "Time Noodles" in English. He stated during a television interview that his dream was to perform ninjobanashi at Carnegie Hall in New York someday and make his audience weep.[129]

On June 7, 2008, the movie theater on the third floor of the Sepra Building in Toyama City was renovated into a 266-seat

---

[127] "9立川志の輔." Wikipedia. Wikimedia Foundation, July 16, 2021.
[128] Kanariya, Eiraku. TATEKAWA SHINOSUKE (立川 志の輔), August 18, 2021.
[129] Kanariya, Eiraku. Anecdotes: Shinosuke, August 19, 2021.

entertainment hall. The management company approached Shinosuke, who was born and raised in Toyama, and asked if they could incorporate his stage name into the hall's name. Shinosuke declined the offer and cited his shyness. However, the hall was eventually named *Teruterutei*, incorporating Shinosuke's real name Teruo. Shinosuke currently holds a rakugo event called Shinosuke's Heart at the hall nearly every month.[130]

He is also well-known as the host of the primetime NHK program *Tameshite Gatten* since it first aired in 1995. Shinosuke brings his sense of humor to the program and helps present cutting-edge research related to health, medicine, and diet in fun, intuitive ways.[131]

---

[130] "立川志の輔." Wikipedia. Wikimedia Foundation, July 16, 2021. https://ja.wikipedia.org/wiki/%E7%AB%8B%E5%B7%9D%E5%BF%97%E3%81%AE%E8%BC%94.

[131] "Shinosuke Tatekawa." Wikipedia. Wikimedia Foundation, July 6, 2021. https://en.wikipedia.org/wiki/Shinosuke_Tatekawa.

xvi. Shunputei Shota (*Photo by Yomiuri Newspaper/Aflo Images*)

16. SHUNPUTEI SHOTA

"I learned that I would learn while teaching my disciples.

Teaching means asking yourself questions and studying."

– Shunputei Shota [132]

Easily recognized as the current host of *Shoten*, Shunputei Shota is a rakugo storyteller, entertainer, actor, and Japanese feudal castle enthusiast.

A Shizuoka native, he is a disciple of Shunputei Ryusho V (1920-2003), a master storyteller who specialized in shinsaku rakugo stories. Ryusho served as an infantryman during the Pacific War (1941-1945) and lost several fingers during a battle. As a result, he turned away from performing koten rakugo stories as they were laden with many expressions using the hands. Shota also performs numerous shinsaku rakugo stories, but he focuses on koten rakugo stories too, which he performs in his own unique style.

Shota's father was a researcher for Nippon Light Metal. His older brother (by two years) enjoyed rakugo since elementary school,

---

[132] "春風亭昇太の言葉 - 経営に効く！名言・格言 今日の一言：楽天ブログ." 楽天ブログ, " August 15, 2012. https://plaza.rakuten.co.jp/madokita/diary/201208150000/.

but Shota himself had no interest in the art of storytelling at that time.

In 1978, he enrolled at Tokai University and accidentally stumbled upon the ochiken when he was seeking out the Latin American Studies group. He ended up becoming an ochiken member simply because it seemed like a fun distraction from his school lessons.

During his second year at the university, he won the *University Rakugo Championship* on television and became a student rakugo master. Afterwards, he appeared on TV Asahi's *The TV Performing Arts* show. In 1982, he dropped out of school and devoted himself to rakugo full-time.

During his training years as a rakugoka, he appeared on many television programs including *Performance Plaza*, on which he served as the host. He was promoted to futatsume in 1986 and adopted the name Shunputei Shota.

Throughout the late 1980s, he continued his television work as an actor and entertainer and was promoted to shinuchi in 1992. In 2003, he founded the *Sosaku Wagei Association* (the Creative Storytelling Association) with Yanagiya Kyotaro, Hayashiya Hikoichi, and Sanyutei Hakucho. In addition, he belongs to the Rakugo Arts Association, a leading association of rakugo performers and other entertainers, and became its president on June 27, 2019.

On May 21, 2006, he joined Nippon Television's *Shoten*. Ten years later, he was appointed the sixth host of the program following former host Katsura Utamaru's retirement.

When the June 30, 2019 episode of *Shoten* concluded, Shota announced that he was finally getting married after years of being ridiculed by the show's other members for his inability to find a wife. During the wedding reception at the Imperial Hotel in Tokyo on October 19, 2019, fellow rakugoka and television personality Shofukutei Tsurube revealed that he had played the role of Cupid in getting the couple together.

Shota is a collector of period items and has a room in his house devoted to such things as old television sets with dials and vintage gramophones. He also likes to collect old cars and currently owns a Rover Mini, a Toyota Publica 800, and a Datsun Bluebird 312.

He is a medieval castle enthusiast and has published various castle-related books, made appearances on related television programs, and given lectures on the topic.

In 2007, he accepted his first disciple, Shunputei Shosho, who is regarded as an *ikemen rakugoka* (handsome rakugoka) in the industry. After accepting Shosho, Shota stated that the experience of having an apprentice can be rather embarrassing. He is a rakugo master who is continually searching for ways to mentor others while keeping his own apprenticeship experiences fresh in his mind.[133]

---

[133] "春風亭昇太." Wikipedia. Wikimedia Foundation, May 2, 2021. https://ja.wikipedia.org/wiki/%E6%98%A5%E9%A2%A8%E4%BA%AD%E6%98%87%E5%A4%AA.

xvii. Yanagiya Kyotaro (*Photo by Yomiuri Newspaper/Aflo Images*)

17. YANAGIYA KYOTARO

"I am really grateful to the audience for coming to my rakugo shows and at the same time, I also feel guilty about it. Yet, the guilt pushes me to try harder.

Rakugo is the last thing people need. They need food, infrastructure, medical care, and transportation first. But living through this pandemic, I really feel that we need to have some fun. Just staying at home is so boring. We need to enjoy our lives. From that perspective, I think what we are doing is important."

— Yanagiya Kyotaro,
Tokyo Kawaraban (September 2021)

Yanagiya Kyotaro is the son of a copywriter who also composed songs under the name of Ohara Yuki. The family called the Okura housing complex in Tokyo's Setagaya Ward home until Kyotaro reached the third grade, after which they moved to Yokohama City. Growing up, Kyotaro loved the *Ultraman* and *Godzilla* films, and is still known as the Ultraman freak in the rakugo world.

Kyotaro became interested in rakugo when he was a junior high school student, and upon enrolling in Nihon University, he joined the rakugo study group there. Taking the stage name of Ieda Raku, he performed rakugo in the streets, at senior citizen's facilities, and even during coming-of-age events to increase his confidence as a storyteller and performer. He worked so hard that he didn't even attend his own coming-of-age ceremony.

He secured a part on a Fuji Television drama while still a college student, but he set aside acting after graduating and took a job at a bookstore. There, he met the woman who would later become his wife.

In retrospect, Kyotaro admitted that he was fearful about pursuing rakugo full-time; however, he could not ignore his passion for the art of storytelling. After about a year and a half of working at the bookstore, he quit his job to pursue rakugo professionally.

He had great admiration for Sanyutei Enjo, who was well-known for his shinsaku rakugo, but he chose Yanagiya Sankyo as his master because he wanted to learn traditional rakugo.

In 1998, Kyotaro was awarded the grand prize in NHK's Newcomer Performing Arts Awards. From that point forward, his popularity increased and he even made an appearance on Nippon Television's *Shoten*. In the years that followed, Kyotaro engaged in a vast array of work in the entertainment industry in addition to performing as a rakugo storyteller. He worked as a voice actor for anime programs, a narrator, a host, an actor, a composer, and a singer. He also served as an advisor for the rakugo-themed anime program, *Descending Stories: Showa Genroku Rakugo Shinju*.[134]

As a rakugoka, his repertoire varies from koten rakugo stories such as "The God of Death" to shinsaku rakugo stories such as "Snow in Hawaii," and he is known to drastically alter the classical stories. One such story is *"Ido no Chawan"* ("Ido's Teacup"). In Kyotaro's version, which he calls *"Utau Ido no Chawan"* ("Singing Ido's Teacup"), all of the characters sing as if in a musical play.

His original story, "Snow in Hawaii," is performed by his master, Sankyo. It is highly unusual for a rakugo master to perform a story written by his disciple. The fact that Sankyo performs Kyotaro's story is an affirmation of his apprentice's creativity and talent.

Other popular, original stories Kyotaro performs include *"Gogo no Hokenshitsu"* ("The School Infirmary in the Afternoon"), *"Sushiya Suikoden"* ("The Story of a Sushi Restaurant"), and *"Nuke Gavadon,"* adapted from *"Nuke Suzume."*

The story *"Gogo no Hokenshitsu"* centers around a school infirmary, where a junior high school student speaks like an old man and the schoolmaster speaks like a young boy.

---

[134] "柳家喬太郎." Wikipedia. Wikimedia Foundation, August 1, 2021. https://ja.wikipedia.org/wiki/%E6%9F%B3%E5%AE%B6%E5%96%AC%E5%A4%AA%E9%83%8E.

"*Sushiya Suikoden*" is adapted from classical Chinese literature and conveys the story of a trained Western chef who is forced to return home and take over his father's sushi restaurant. He is left alone at the restaurant after all the sushi chefs quit and is required to make sushi by himself. Unfortunately, he is so bad at making sushi that some of his clientele actually step behind the counter and help him. In the end, he has to close the restaurant because he cannot afford to pay his client's salaries.

"*Nuke Suzume*" means a sparrow coming out of a folding screen. In the original story, a hotel guest, who has no money to pay for his room, paints images of sparrows on the inn's folding screen as repayment. The painting is so realistic that the sparrows emerge from the screen and fly out of the room every morning, only to return later and become a part of the screen once again. Word of the phenomenon spreads throughout Japan. Guests flock to the rundown little inn and the inn owner becomes wealthy. In his adaptation, Kyotaro changes the sparrow to a Gavadon, a giant monster created when a child's graffiti of the creature is brought to life by strange cosmic rays. The monster is eventually detained by Ultraman, taken to outer space, and changed into a constellation.[135]

Kyotaro is also known for performing stories that have all but disappeared from the world of rakugo. Some of the stories he has

---

[135] Kanariya, Eiraku. YANAGIYA KYOTARO (柳家喬太郎), August 21, 2021.

revived include "*Wata Isha*" ("Cotton Doctor"), "*Giboshi*" ("Bronze Ornament"), and "*Nishikino Maiginu*" ("Silk Dancing Outfit").

In the story "*Wata Isha*," a patient is rushed to the doctor's office complaining of stomach pains. To solve the problem, the doctor replaces the patient's innards with cotton and the patient is cured.

"*Giboshi*" is about a young master suffering from depression. His worried parents hire a male geisha, who helps him overcome his depression by erecting scaffolding near the five-storied pagoda in Asakusa, which allows the young master to climb to the top and lick the pagoda's bronze ornament. It turns out that his inability to lick the bronze ornament was the cause of his depression.

"*Nishikino Maiginu*" is a story adapted by Sanyutei Encho based on the French play "La Tosca" written by Victorien Sardou.

Kyotaro's makura are just as masterful as his stories, and he is regarded as the virtuoso of the makura along with the late Yanagiya Kosanji and Tatekawa Shinosuke.

He is a rakugoka who advocates listening to rakugo over reading about it. He once said, "If you can't enjoy it without knowing all there is to know about it, it must be dull rakugo."[136]

---

[136] "柳家喬太郎." Wikipedia.

xviii. Olympic Torchbearer Katsura Bunshi V, Tokyo, 2020. (*Photo by Kazuki Oishi / Alamy Stock Photo*)

18. KATSURA BUNSHI VI

"It is impossible for my life to be completed.

For example, reaching retirement age does not mean that life is complete."

— Katsura Bunshi VI

Propelled to superstardom by the thriving television and late-night radio industries, Katsura Bunshi is a prominent Kamigata rakugo storyteller and television personality. The third disciple of one of the celebrated postwar rakugo greats, Katsura Bunshi V, he appeared under the stage name of Katsura Sanshi for 45 years until he succeeded to the stage name of his master and became the sixth generation Katsura Bunshi in 2012.

As a member of the new generation of rakugo storytellers, and highly influenced by rakugoka Sanyutei Enjo in Tokyo, Bunshi has been more interested in composing new stories than learning Kamigata rakugo's traditional repertoire. He and his fellow young rakugo performers wanted to create rakugo with which people in their generation could identify. As a result, in 2020, the number of new shinsaku rakugo stories Bunshi created reached 300. However, he does not like to refer to these stories as "new" stories (as opposed to classical koten rakugo stories) and prefers to call them *creative stories.*

Many of his creative stories have been performed by other rakugoka, including Osaka rakugo performer Diane Kichijitsu,[137] and Bunshi's Canadian disciple, Katsura Sunshine, who also translates his master's work into English. Some of Bunshi's memorable original stories include "*Owasuremono Uketamawari Jo*" ("The Lost and Found Office"), "*Shukudai*" ("Homework"), "*Umare Kawari*" ("Reincarnation"), and "*Gorufu yoake mae*" ("Golf Before Dawn"). "Golf Before Dawn" was awarded the Agency for Cultural Affairs Art Festival Grand Prize in 1983.[138]

The story "Lost and Found Office" is perhaps the one most often performed in English by other rakugo performers. It centers around the conversations between an agent of the lost and found office at a train station and a man claiming to have left his umbrella on the train. The repartee between the characters and the build up to the punchline is a true testament to Bunshi's genius.

For a man whose job is to make people laugh, Bunshi's early life was fraught with tragedy. Bunshi was only 11 months old when his father, who worked as a bank clerk at Nomura Bank, passed

---

[137] "Rakugo." Rakugo | ダイアン吉日 Diane Kichijitsu, 2014. http://www.diane-o.com/rakugo.
[138] "ゴルフ夜明け前." Wikipedia. Wikimedia Foundation, July 28, 2021.
https://ja.wikipedia.org/wiki/%E3%82%B4%E3%83%AB%E3%83%95%E5%A4%9C%E6%98%8E%E3%81%91%E5%89%8D.

away from tuberculosis. Afterwards, the father's side of the family pressured Bunshi's mother to leave the baby with them. She refused and went into hiding in the Taisho Ward in Osaka City. In 1950, Osaka was hit by a typhoon that caused substantial damage to Bunshi's home. The following year, a fire swept through the Taisho Ward, completely destroying their residence. As a result, very few photographs remain of Bunshi at a young age.[139]

In April 1959, Bunshi entered the Osaka City Ichioka Commercial High School. While still a high school student, he appeared on ABC Radio's *Manzai Classroom* with his fellow classmates and managed to win the prize money. He enrolled in Kansai University's Department of Commerce in 1963 and joined the Kansai University Rakugo Study Group the following year. He delighted his friends and fellow students by performing rakugo under the stage name of Romantei Chikku.

Bunshi dropped out of school to become a disciple of Katsura Bunshi V in 1966. While studying rakugo, he became a regular on MBS Radio's *Sing! MBS Youngtown*. He continued to work regularly on radio and television, eventually becoming the disciple

---

[139] "桂文枝 (6代目)." Wikipedia. Wikimedia Foundation, July 16, 2021. https://ja.wikipedia.org/wiki/%E6%A1%82%E6%96%87%E6%9E%9D_(6%E4%BB%A3%E7%9B%AE).

who appeared most often on television programs in the Katsura Bunshi rakugo family.[140]

Although he emerged as an entertainer early in life, he was not rated very highly as a rakugoka initially. It wasn't until, taking inspiration from Sanyutei Enjo, he began to emphasize new creative stories over the classics that his rating as a rakugoka soared. Throughout the first half of the 1990s, he was the number one ranked entertainer in the Kansai area. With the beginning of the 21st century, however, his popularity as a television personality began to wane and he turned his attention to his main art, rakugo.

At one point, Bunshi considered running in the House of Councilors election in 1995 and held a press conference to announce his intentions. His artistic family was opposed to it so he eventually gave up the idea.

In 2003, at the age of 60, he became the sixth president of the Kamigata Rakugo Association and served until his resignation in 2018. He returned to the Association as a special advisor in June 2020. Recently, he was the only rakugo storyteller to serve on the Culture and Education Commission of the 2020 Tokyo Olympic and Paralympic Games.[141]

---

[140] "Yoshimoto Company (Katsura Bunshi Biography)." 吉本興業株式会社. Accessed August 17, 2021. http://www.yoshimoto.co.jp/bunshi/biography.html.
[141] "桂文枝 (6代目)." Wikipedia.

In 2015, he received recognition from Guinness World Records as the exclusive host of the longest-running TV talk show, *Shinkon-san Irasshai!* (*Welcome Newlyweds!*). He began hosting the program on TV Asahi in January 1971, and the year 2021 marked the 50th anniversary of the program.

Each week, two newlywed couples are invited to the studio to talk about their love lives. Often the discussions lapse into grievances about one another, giving Bunshi a chance to react with comic exaggeration. The show has hosted over 4,500 couples to date.[142]

Bunshi is also an avid *shogi* player (Japanese chess) and is currently ranked 5th dan in the amateur ranking system. Amateur shogi players are ranked from 10 kyu to 1 kyu and then from 1 dan to 7 dan.[143]

---

[142] "Veteran TV Host Katsura Lauded by Guinness for 45-Year Run." The Japan Times, July 3, 2015. https://www.japantimes.co.jp/culture/2015/07/03/entertainment-news/bunshi-katsura-sets-guinness-record-45-year-run-tv-shows-host/.
[143] "桂文枝 (6代目)." Wikipedia.

The Interviews

xix. Katsura Fukuryu (*Photo by Kaya Ogata*)

19. KATSURA FUKURYU

"Rakugoka are like Japanese 'ryokan' or 'traditional inns.'

A ryokan tries to figure out the needs of the guest by reading the atmosphere and then providing what they think the customer needs. This is how successful professional rakugoka work as well. Reading the atmosphere is essential!"

– Katsura Fukuryu [144]

Canadian Katsura Fukuryu made Japan his home in 2001. He was managing his own English conversation learning center when he was introduced to the rakugo of Kamigata rakugo legend, Katsura Shijaku. From that point forward, Fukuryu has pursued the path that eventually led him to the world of professional rakugo.

He began his performing career by joining an amateur English rakugo club. He performed English rakugo for several years under the stage name of Duke KanaDA. His clever *kozamei* (stage name) was derived by combining the meaning of his real first name with the Japanese word *kanata*, meaning "beyond" or "far off (in the distance)," and adding the *nonoten* (ditto mark) to turn "ta" into "da." Fukuryu's real first name means "gifted ruler," and kanata was an appropriate choice for a Canadian living and performing

---

[144] Katsura, Fukuryu. Email interview with the author, September 24, 2021.

in a distant land. It also sounds very similar to his place of birth, Canada.

In October 2016, he became the 11th disciple of rakugo master Katsura Fukudanji. He was the first and only foreign disciple of the then 76-year-old master, who accepted him after refraining from taking apprentices for over ten years. As tradition dictates, Fukudanji selected the stage name for his apprentice. He coined the name *Fukuryu* by blending the letters of his own kozamei with the first part of his disciple's former stage name, "Du." However, since the sound "du" does not exist in the Japanese language, "ryu," and meaning "dragon," was substituted.[145]

KO: You were born and raised in Winnipeg, Canada and your love of Japan and Japanese culture brought you to Japan. How were you initially introduced to Japanese culture when you lived in Canada?

KF: *During my first year of high school, the school piloted a Japanese language course for the first time. I immediately took an interest in the course.*

As a junior high student, I had a recurring nightmare over a period of several months, but I didn't know what it meant.

---

[145] Katsura, Fukuryu, phone conversation with the author, October 27, 2021.

After I joined the Japanese language class, I told my Japanese language teacher about my dream, and she knew immediately! She unexpectedly said, "That's Sekigahara!"[146] I finally understood that my nightmare was about Japan. That realization made me even more interested in Japan and its culture.

Originally, I had planned to finish my last year of high school in Japan by taking part in the Rotary Club Exchange program. Out of 500 applicants, they narrowed the candidates down to the final two. I was one of the final two. However, since they could only send one of us to Japan and couldn't decide which one to choose, they had a coin toss, and I lost.

I finished high school and university in Canada, but I vowed to travel to Japan on my own someday. Finally, on September 21, 2001, I realized my dream and journeyed to Japan.

KO: You mentioned that you came to Japan on September 21, 2001, ten days after the 9-11 tragedy. As I recall, the

---

[146] Sekigahara: A rural town in the Chubu region of Japan where the epic battle between Tokugawa Ieyasu (the first Shogun of the Tokugawa shogunate) and Ishida Mitsunari took place.

aviation industry was in absolute chaos at the time, what was it like to travel under such circumstances?[147]

Also, how did you happen to pick that specific time to travel to Japan? Was there something about the event itself that triggered your decision to come to Japan?

KF: *I had been planning to come to Japan for more than a year. At the time, I was very scared to fly, mostly because I had never been outside of North America before, but I was also determined to carry out my dream. My mother didn't want me to go, but I'm very stubborn that way.*

I left for Japan 10 days after 9-11. My parents drove me to the airport to see me off. Going through security was very scary and overwhelming as it took around three hours to get through. I remember there were only three of us on the flight to Vancouver. The two flight attendants came in and out of hiding from time to time to check on us.

In Vancouver, the transition to my international flight went more smoothly. I think I was the only non-Japanese person on

---

[147] The September 11 attacks also commonly referred to as 9/11, were a series of four coordinated terrorist attacks by the militant Islamist terrorist group al-Qaeda against the United States on the morning of Tuesday, September 11, 2001.

the flight. I assumed everyone else just wanted to go home. This time, the flight was full.

We got to the runway and were about to take off, but the pilot came on the PA and announced that we had a problem and we needed to go back to the terminal! Everyone was in a panic, but we tried to stay calm. We returned to the terminal and everyone was asked to disembark. Afterwards, they proceeded to re-scan all of our tickets. Apparently, they had done a head count on the plane before takeoff and realized that there was one extra passenger on board. After our tickets were rescanned, we reboarded the plane and took off three hours later than expected.

KO: Most foreigners who come to Japan take up teaching English, and you chose that path while learning Japanese. How did you make the leap from teaching to rakugo?

KF: I worked for an Eikaiwa-style (English conversation) company teaching English to children. After two and a half years with the organization, I started my own business doing the same thing.

Then in 2011, a friend asked me if I knew what rakugo was. I said "Zabuton Ichimai?"[148] She said, "No! Those are rakugo performers, but they are playing a kind of game show (ogiri)." She proceeded to pull out her smartphone and showed me a video of Katsura Shijaku, the pioneer of English rakugo. Although he was performing rakugo in Japanese on that particular video, I found it very interesting. She told me that if I had any interest in rakugo, she would introduce me to an amateur English rakugo club she was familiar with.

That is how I started my journey into the world of rakugo.

KO: You made reference to the TV show *Shoten*. How did you know about it? Were you exposed to it in Japan or Canada?

KF: I did watch some Japanese TV in Winnipeg. The programs were prerecorded by people with satellite televisions and donated to the Japanese Cultural Centre. I primarily watched the NHK taiga dramas (historical fiction television series); however, there was possibly an episode or two of Shoten among the programs.

---

[148] Reference to the television show Shoten.

I did watch Shoten from time to time when I came to Japan. I didn't always understand it at first, but it was definitely good for my listening skills.

KO: Your bio indicates that you had show business experience in Canada. Can you elaborate on that?

KF: *I attended magic school in Canada since I was 6 years old. I advanced to the professional level in magic and balloon art. I love all kinds of magic; however, my favorite types are close-up and escape magic.*

I love close-up magic because you can talk and interact with the audience. I performed at events, conferences, trade shows, and of course busking. I have been told that I was a talker since I was a baby! And I think magic helped me become a good storyteller.

KO: You said that you joined an amateur English rakugo club and began performing rakugo in English. Did you translate the stories you performed yourself, or did you have access to translated scripts through the English rakugo club?

KF: *I translated the stories myself, but I did have a lot of help, especially with koten rakugo. There are many words that were new and unfamiliar to me.*

KO: You became the 11th disciple of Katsura Fukudanji in October 2016 because you wanted to study Japanese rakugo. Not too many Japanese rakugo masters accept foreign apprentices. Did you have a difficult time persuading him to take you on? Why did you choose Fukudanji specifically?

KF: *I regularly met Katsura Fukudanji, before he became my master, at a local izakaya where he performed several times a year. I met him at other places as well; however, at the izakaya, I actually had the chance to talk to him and get to know him better after the show since he stayed for the after-parties.*

At first, I didn't bother to ask him to be my master because I heard that he was not taking on new apprentices and was only concentrating on performing. As time went on, after I had been performing English rakugo for several years as a professional, we met again at the izakaya after the show. It was the summer of 2016, and he was curious about English rakugo. He had never seen English rakugo being performed.

He said to me, "The stage is open! Go do English rakugo!" I thought, "NOW?" I must have actually said it aloud because he said, "Yes! Now!" At the time, I was not wearing a kimono, and went on stage wearing an aloha shirt!

I performed a ten-minute version of "Jugemu." I must have impressed him because he said, "You should have the Katsura name!"

I thought, "Is this my chance? Why not?" I mustered up all of my courage and asked, "Would you be my master?" and he said, "Yes!" So after ten years of not accepting apprentices, he took on a foreigner as his 11th apprentice.

KO: How would you describe your experiences as an apprentice? Even those who are born and raised in Japan have a difficult time adjusting to the master-apprentice system. Were you able to make the transition easily?

KF: *I performed apprentice duties for many rakugo masters for several years in order to find out what it would be like to be an apprentice. However, I never actually got the title of apprentice even though that's literally what I was doing.*

It was no different for me than it was for any other apprentice. It may have even been harder in some cases as I had to prove myself every day!

I was once told to think of the original three-year training time as a prison sentence. It'll be hell for three years, but you know you have a release date.

As I did have some experience with apprentice duties, I didn't have as much trouble with things like technique, etc. that some others may have had.

KO: You mentioned that you performed apprentice duties, but you were not an "official" apprentice at the time. How did that come about?

KF: I am someone who believes that when opportunity knocks, then I should answer it! If possible, I like to know what I'm getting into before committing to something.

Over time, I had the opportunity to meet many professional rakugoka. I met one of them in Yokkaichi. He was performing with a friend who performs English rakugo. We met after the show, and he asked me if I wanted to become his apprentice. We stayed in contact while I waited for him to get permission *from his master to take an apprentice of his own. In the meantime, I performed various apprentice duties for him.*

I waited more than three years; however, nothing came of it. Since I wasn't an actual "apprentice" to any one master, I got to know and help other masters as well.

KO: I understand that you also perform rakugo in sign language. At one point in his career, your master injured his throat and lost his voice temporarily. During that period, he learned sign language and started using it to perform rakugo. How influential was your master in your decision to learn sign language rakugo? How often do you perform in sign language?

KF: *My master was extremely influential in my decision to learn sign language.*

On my first day helping my master, I met him and his manager at the train station. I actually met his manager at the station first. My master was on the second floor of a restaurant looking out the window at us. He was signing with the manager. I thought to myself how useful sign language was.

One of my rakugo brothers, who is deaf and has just earned the name of Fukudanjitei Fukuichi (formerly Fukudango), was another huge influence in my decision to learn JSL (Japanese Sign Language). He doesn't have the Katsura family name because he can't speak, and he is only able to perform rakugo using sign language.

The first time that we met was at a "Laughing Matsuri" at Hiraoka Jinja! It was the first time I saw him perform sign language rakugo! Since many people don't understand sign language, one of my other brothers, Katsura Fukuroku, stood beside the stage and translated while Fukuichi performed.

Before the pandemic, I performed sign language rakugo with my master and Fukuichi all over Japan. I performed one sign language rakugo show for every 10 English and Japanese rakugo shows before the pandemic. Since the pandemic began, I have performed one sign language rakugo show for every 40+ English and Japanese rakugo shows.

KO: Due to the pandemic, you have been performing online quite a bit. You even performed with Sanyutei Koseinen allowing your audience to experience the charm of both Kamigata and Edo-Tokyo rakugo.

Rakugo performers typically rely on audience response to gauge their performance. How difficult was it to transition to an online performance where you are speaking to a camera and not getting that instant feedback you are so accustomed to?

KF: *The pandemic changed the way the world thinks and acts. Rakugo is no different. When everything was shut down, we had to come up with new ideas to stay alive! Online rakugo seemed to be the way. It has been a challenge to switch to online rakugo. Especially trying to make a living doing it!*

Online performances make it very difficult to gauge the audience's mood as we cannot see or hear them. Gauging the audience is very important for a rakugoka. That's what our "makura" or "pillow talk" is used for before performing the appropriate story for the audience.

Rakugoka are like Japanese "ryokan" or "traditional inns." A ryokan tries to figure out the needs of the guest by reading the atmosphere and then providing what they think the customer needs. This is how successful professional rakugoka work as well. Reading the atmosphere is essential! Online rakugo makes that nearly impossible. However, rakugoka are masters at adapting.

KO: I thought it was very interesting that you had experience as a busker. Knowing that Kamigata rakugo actually started out as a street art, I found this connection very interesting. It seems that you were destined to become a Kamigata rakugoka all along! Do you have, or plan to take on, your own apprentices?

KF: *I appreciate your connection of how Kamigata rakugo started to busking in Canada. I also agree that I was destined to become a Kamigata rakugoka. Busking and storytelling both come naturally to me.*

As for apprentices, I've been given permission from my master to take on apprentices and would like to do so sometime in the future. My son just turned 2 years old and is already a talker. I do dream of the day when he becomes my apprentice. However, that is his decision — when he is ready to make that choice!

xx. Katsura Utzao (*Photo courtesy of Katsura Utazo*)

20. KATSURA UTAZO

"Rakugo is like words written in the wind. It could be recorded on video or audio, but the realm created by the storyteller remains only in the memory of the audience."

— Katsura Utazo [149]

Rakugo master Katsura Utamaru, best known for hosting Nippon Television's Shoten, trained five disciples in his lifetime. Storyteller Katsura Utazo was one of them. Utazo once entertained the idea of becoming a professional musician, but he surrendered that dream in December 1991 to become a rakugo storyteller.

His current dream is to become an international storyteller and perpetuate the art of rakugo beyond the borders of Japan. A highly versatile individual, he is the only rakugoka to hold a professional boxing Class C license, which he earned in 1994.[150]

> **KO:** Before you became a disciple of Katsura Utamaru, you traveled to England to join the karate dojo run by Jean-Jacques Burnell, a member of the British punk rock band The Stranglers. You also earned a professional boxing

---

[149] Katsura, Utazo. Email interview with the author, September 27, 2021.
[150] Allred, Laurie. "Rakugo Master Utazo Katsura to Share Traditional Japanese Storytelling in English." Daily Bruin, February 24, 2012.
https://dailybruin.com/2012/02/24/rakugo_master_utazo_katsura_to_share_traditional_japanese_storytelling_in_english.

Class C license in 1994. Both music and sports appear to be your hobbies, but did you ever want to become a professional athlete or musician?

KU: *I came to Tokyo when I was a college student with the dream of becoming a professional musician. I surrendered that dream when I was 26 and became a rakugo storyteller instead.*

I obtained my professional boxing license during my zenza years. After I earned my license as a boxer, I once again attempted to become a musician and stop training in rakugo. But I eventually abandoned my pursuit and continued as a storyteller.

KO: How did you meet Jean-Jacques Burnell?

KU: *When I was a high school student, I learned the same style of karate that he had studied. In my college years, one of his female fans introduced me to him and I decided to go to England.*

KO: When and why did you decide to enter the world of rakugo?

KU: *I decided to enter the world of rakugo after I returned from England. It was such an invigorating experience that I wanted to talk about it.*

KO: You were born in Sakai City, Osaka, but you did not choose to pursue Kamigata rakugo. Why?

KU: *I have loved rakugo ever since I was a small child. During my high school years, I was a huge fan of Katsura Shijaku, a master of Kamigata rakugo. To this day, he is my favorite rakugo performer. But, Shijaku said that he would no longer take on disciples, so I decided to become a rakugo performer in Tokyo.*

KO: You asked to become Utamaru shisho's disciple. Why did you choose him as your master?

KU: *At that time, I was living in Machida City and my master's home was located in Yokohama. I thought I could easily commute to his house during my training. However, I became a live-in apprentice and I moved to my master's house in Yokohama.*

KO: I understand that you serve as a moderator and reporter for martial arts broadcasts. How do you connect martials arts and rakugo in your life?

KU: *There are some common elements shared between the two disciplines, such as demonstrating a respect for civility, adherence to traditional rituals, and the existence of a hierarchical system. But I don't really dwell on these things too much.*

KO: Since 2005, you have toured many countries, including Thailand, Brazil, India, Kazakhstan, The United States, and even Sakhalin as a rakugo performer. What drew you to these foreign countries to perform rakugo?

KU: *I became a rakugo performer after returning to Japan from England. It has always been my dream to become an international storyteller – one who can perform overseas.*

KO: You began performing English rakugo in 2010. Prior to that, when you toured foreign countries, did you perform strictly in Japanese? With subtitles?

KU: *In the beginning, I performed rakugo in Japanese without subtitles for Japanese audiences overseas. Afterwards, I started performing rakugo in English in English-speaking countries. I only performed rakugo using subtitles in non-English speaking countries.*

KO: Although rakugo is still not very well known overseas, in an interview you gave to the Daily Bruin in 2012, you said, "I enjoyed English rakugo overseas much more than Japanese rakugo." Why?

KU: *It is because I became a rakugo performer after experiencing a different culture abroad. The environment overseas is much more unrestricted than here in Japan. I still recall the culture shock I experienced in England.*

KO: You are also a writer and you have won several writing awards. I understand that you prefer to perform koten rakugo stories. Have you written any original rakugo stories?

KU: *I wrote a few stories when I was a futatsume. These days, I occasionally make changes to koten stories and insert my original ideas into the introduction.*

KO: Do you have a specific goal you would like to achieve as a rakugo performer? What would you like your legacy to be?

KU: *I want to live as long as possible and live a life where I can entertain many people.*

Rakugo is like words written in the wind. It could be recorded on video or audio, but the realm created by the storyteller remains only in the memory of the audience. On the other hand, texts such as novels remain preserved and unaltered.

I want to do both.

21. STÉPHANE FERRANDEZ

"Just as it is difficult to leave the zabuton, once one starts to do rakugo, it was difficult for me to stop storytelling once I graduated."

– Stéphane Ferrandez[151]

Stéphane Ferrandez describes himself as an ethnologist, storyteller, and rakugo performer. He is the 2009 Villa Kujoyama laureate and the co-founder of La Cie Balabolka.

Villa Kujoyama is an artists' residence in Kyoto, Japan that is managed by the Institut Français du Japon. It offers personalized support to the French and Japanese artists in residence while promoting interdisciplinarity arts and cultural exchange. It is one of the largest French cultural institutions abroad, and is the only one of its kind in Asia. La Cie Balabolka was founded in 2006 by Stéphane and author/director Sandrine Garbuglia. This organization endeavors to perpetuate age-old stories from around the world.

In 2019, Stéphane, Sandrine, and Cyril Coppini (another French rakugo performer) released *Histoires tombées d'un éventail (Stories Fallen from a Fan)*. The book provides an overview of rakugo and

---

[151] Stéphane Ferrandez. Email interview with the author, December 1, 2021.

introduces readers to various prominent rakugo storytellers including Henry Black (Kairakutei Black), Katsura Utamaru, and Katsura Koharudanji. The work also includes several well-liked rakugo stories translated into French. [152]

KO: You describe yourself as an ethnologist, storyteller and rakugo performer. How did you become interested in studying different human cultures?

SF: *Since childhood, like many children, I loved stories about magic and adventure. Stories about explorers and investigators who were traveling around the world trying to solve mysteries, find treasure, or save humankind. That's the thrill I was seeking.*

I decided to become an ethnologist while in junior high school because I wanted to travel to other nations and meet different people. I wanted to understand their views about life and learn from their customs and culture. At the same time, I discovered the power of theater and the joy of performing on stage.

---

[152] "RAKUGO FRANCE-Équipe." RAKUGO FRANCE - Équipe, 2021. http://www.rakugo.fr/%C3%A9quipe/.

Wishing to combine these two passions, I choose to study storytelling by interviewing professional storytellers who were conveying stories from their country or area of origin.

Later on, for my degree, I researched what health impact folktales and the manner of telling them had on an audience. Twenty-five years ago, the effect of storytelling on people with Alzheimer's and Autism was just being tested and surveyed. To understand the impact, I began learning stories and conveying them myself.

Just as it is difficult to leave the zabuton, once one starts to do rakugo, it was difficult for me to stop storytelling once I graduated. Consequently, I decided to become an actor and a storyteller. My training as an ethnologist helped me to transmit the traditional tales from other countries while respecting their culture.

KO: When did you first become interested in Japan and Japanese culture?

SF: *Sometimes a story begins with the attention given to a simple detail or an object that eventually leads the character to make certain choices in life.*

I think my fascination with Japan began when I saw a Japanese doll inside a glass case for the first time. It was a gift given to my grandmother by her globetrotting friends. Oftentimes, I stared intently at the image of Kinkakuji, the Golden Temple, that was painted in front of the delicate silhouette of the geisha doll who was looking out toward the very spot I had the opportunity to gaze upon two decades later. This object stamped "Made in Japan," highly influenced my young dreams.

During my childhood, I also saw a lot of anime such as Robo Grendizer, Gatchaman, Galaxy 999, and more. As a teenager, I watched Space Kobura and movies about Japan's history and culture like Akira Kurosawa's Seven Samurai.

In high school, I tried to learn the basic rudiments of Japanese writing and reading using some of the rare books that were published then. These days, I'm still studying Japanese, frequenting different French-Japanese meetings or events, and participating in some classes when I am not on tour.

KO: You became the 2009 laureate of the prestigious Villa Kujoyama in Kyoto. How did you become involved with Villa Kujoyama? How long were you there?

SF: *My story is one that I share with Sandrine Garbuglia. She adapts our rakugo stories and without her astuteness, talent for writing, and her director's eye, it would have been difficult to bring these rakugo stories to the stage.*

During our first trip to Japan in 2007, we both became a little obsessed with rakugo after seeing Shoten on TV at a friend's house in Kumamoto. We wanted to know more about this amazing talking art. Back in France, one day, Sandrine came across Ian Mc Arthur's thesis about Henry Black (Kairakutei Black) on the internet. He was the first foreigner to become a shinuchi during the Meiji era and together with Sanyutei Encho I, made significant contributions to the world of rakugo. The romanticism which characterized his life drew us closer to rakugo culture. We wanted to trace Henry's footsteps with the aim of creating a play about his life and his stories.

We thought that Villa Kujoyama would provide us with the ideal opportunity to meet rakugo storytellers. We sent our proposed project to the judges, were selected, and we won. It was as if Henry's spirit wanted us to come to Japan. We first explored iromono and spent more than six months in Kyoto.

Living at Villa Kujoyama — an incredible contemporary house bordered by traditional Japanese houses, isolated on Kujoyama Hill with monkeys and wild boars as our neighbors — was a great opportunity to discover, feel, and live the Japanese way of life. In time, we also learned quite a bit from rakugoka in Osaka.

KO: What appealed to you most about rakugo? Who did you study rakugo with? Where and for how long?

SF: *As a storyteller and a trained comedian, I always mixed gesture, dialogue, and narration during my performances. About 15 years ago, some of my fellow storytellers told me that I was more a showman doing stand-up than a raconteur. Imagine my surprise when I saw a hanashika doing all the same things I was doing to give life to his story. As Japanese storytellers always say, "It is sit down comedy."*

I wanted to learn more about the rakugo tales and techniques. I had been initiated to Puppet Theater and had learned mime techniques, so rakugo seemed to be the ideal art through which I could mix all the different elements to give life to a story.

In 2009, together with Sandrine, I studied rakugo in Osaka with Katsura Asakichi and Hayashiya Someta. They had both performed rakugo in English in Europe and the United States. Our lessons took place in a room near Tenma Tenjin Hanjotei, Osaka's yose theater. We also utilized Hayashiya Someta's rehearsal room near Minami Tenma Park.

We studied with Katsura Asakichi-san through January 2010. He served as our guide and master — revealing a new story, a new piece of information, a new rule, or a new gesture each time we met.

Our first lesson will always be our most memorable. In France, we were accustomed to hearing a little story before beginning a storytelling course; however, the unexpected happened with Asakichi-san. He began by showing us the Japanese kimono and other traditional clothing and said, "Now, you will first learn how to fold a kimono, a haori, a juban, etc... After that, you will learn how to wear a kimono and tie your obi."

It was only at the end of the session that he taught us a very short story — funny and also poetic — a kokkeibanashi called "Uekiya, the Gardener."

In the fall, we collaborated with Hayashiya Someta. We even had the opportunity to share the stage together. He joined us for an evening party, a rendezvous with Kujoyama's artists and creators, which takes place twice a year. He began telling the story "Toki Udon" in Japanese, and I finished it in French. I also performed "Uekiya, the Gardener" in Japanese. The show attracted more than 200 spectators. We noticed then the strength and appeal of rakugo.

With Sandrine, we created a big rakugo event at the Kyoto French Institute in December. Katsura Asakichi, Diane Kichijitsu and the shamisen player, Teranishi Miki, shared the stage with us.

I performed "Tameshizake" for the first time. It is one of Henry Black's famous koten rakugo stories. As Asakichi-san had advised me, the public will applaud when you empty your sakazuki (a container that is used for drinking Japanese sake), if you drink well, and they did.

I think when a zenza experiences such a moment, he may feel like a real rakugoka at last. That's the feeling I had as a performer daring to follow in Henry Black's footsteps.

We did five rakugo tours in Japan between 2012 and 2018. Each trip served as a means to learn new stories with Hayashiya Someta and interview great storytellers from Kamigata and Edo/Tokyo. We interviewed Shunputei Shota,

> *Sanyutei Enraku VI, and a few other participants from the television program Shoten.*

KO: Is there a Japanese rakugo performer whom you admire and who has influenced you the most as a performer?

SF: *Katsura Shijaku is the name that always springs to mind. Actually, I admire several rakugoka including, Yanagiya Kosan V, Katsura Beicho, Katsura Utamaru, Yanagiya Kosanji, Katsura Koharudanji, and Shunputei Shota. They have all influenced me.*

I think what I admire the most about them is that they each have their own unique and distinct style of storytelling.

Each hanashika is a great source of fun and learning. Each gesture, tone of voice, accent, or a certain way of performing can add so much flavor to a story

KO: You seem passionate about Asia and about spreading rakugo outside the borders of Japan. You and Sandrine Garbuglia translate/ adapt traditional rakugo tales into French. How many stories have you adapted to date? How do you select which stories to translate?

SF: *We adapted more than 30 stories so far. We still have more waiting in a box.*

As Japan-fanatics, we want to reach as many people who are unfamiliar with this extraordinary culture as we can.

We usually select stories that humorously mock and present with a certain tenderness the shortcomings common to our human condition whether we live in Japan or in France. Our goal is to entice our spectators to have fun and laugh while listening to the story where the characters exhibit universal flaws and qualities.

We do not select stories where the punchline or the wordplay will be lost in translation. These types of stories require a thorough understanding of Japanese culture and its many idioms.

Sometimes, you have to be Japanese to fully appreciate a rakugo story. Sometimes, it appears that a story cannot be translated, but if you wait a while, you can successfully adapt it. We waited around 10 years before adapting "Atama Yama" ("Head Mountain.")

KO: You have performed in many cities including Paris, Kyoto, and Tokyo. Do you find that audiences in France prefer different types of stories compared to audiences in Japan, for instance?

SF: *In France, there was a time when it was funny to speak about our neighbors like the Belgians, or for a Parisian, about the inhabitants of the South or North of France, mocking their accent, manner of speaking, and their strange habits. It's rude, isn't it? No place for that in 2021!*

But we can still laugh about ourselves as we do in stand-up comedy, and we like it. Sandrine also enjoys adapting some stories with strong female characters.

Among the rakugo stories that can't easily be adapted are the ones which focus on the differences in dialect and customs/habits between Edo/Tokyo residents and Kamigata residents, for example.

It's really difficult to translate in another language all the subtleties, the hierarchical way of speaking, or dialects like kansai-ben or fukuoka-ben.

What I mean by this is that mocking our universal shortcomings will always be a better choice when trying to elicit laughter. In this way, audiences in France like the same kinds of stories the Japanese audiences enjoy. Maybe, the manga fans will prefer kaidanbanashi or strange tales where humans are confronted by yokai like in "Yume Hachi" or "Shinigami." But all classic rakugo stories such as "Toki Udon," "Hatsu Tenjin," or "The Zoo" always find their way into the hearts of the public.

In Japan, during one of our rakugo tours, we adapted French, African, and Brazilian stories for rakugo. These stories were examples of how laughter can be universal. Presenting these stories in the rakugo style was a good way to introduce the Japanese audiences to the many folktales from around the world.

I also presented the Senegalese tale "Diabou N'Dao," while playing the Kalimba (the African thumb piano). The audience was very intrigued and enthused to discover this instrument.

KO: You are also a multi-instrumentalist who has mastered various instruments from the five continents. Have you always been interested in music or did your interest evolve as you began to explore different cultures, weaving their stories and music into your studies and performances?

SF: *I have always been fond of music. I started to learn to play the guitar (blues in particular) when I was in high school. I discovered the pleasure of playing percussion instruments (djembe, pandeiro, kalimba and later Shamisen) through my association with cultural and theatrical organizations, where I met people from Brazil, Africa, Maghreb, and in recent years from Japan.*

KO: What do you envision for the future of rakugo? Will you create your own rakugo stories someday?

SF: *For the future, I envision that rakugo will gain wider acceptance around the world. Katsura Sunshine's rakugo show on Broadway last year is about to resume in New York and will also be presented in London. I feel that this is proof of rakugo's success.*

Actually there is already a rise in the popularity of rakugo. For nearly 12 years now, I have been working with Sandrine to spread the knowledge about rakugo – doing a lot of lectures and shows in France and Europe. During the last couple of years, we noticed that a lot of people have heard about rakugo through manga, anime, and articles.

One of my greatest dreams is to set up a big rakugokai where I could perform rakugo in French and English with all the foreign rakugoka such as Katsura Sunshine, Sanyutei Koseinin, Diane Kichijitsu, Warattei Harito, and others who are accustomed to performing in English or using subtitles, like Kanariya Eishi, Katsura Koharudanji, Hayashiya Someta, Katsura Kaishi.

Sandrine has created countless makura for our shows in France and in Japan. We still have a lot of work ahead of us. We enjoy discovering, learning and adapting koten rakugo, and we have never considered writing shinsaku story in French.

Maybe for our next tour in Japan when better days come.

xxi. Kanariya Koraku (*Photo by Kanariya Kichiyu*)

22. KANARIYA KORAKU

"Speaking a different language is like living someone else's life or having another persona within you."

— *Kanariya Koraku* [153]

Kanariya Koraku is a multi-faceted and multi-talented rakugo performer whose storytelling style is imbued with versatility nurtured by his many experiences overseas. He is a devoted linguist and aspires to become Japan's first multilingual rakugo performer.

A former diplomat, he performs rakugo for Japanese and foreign audiences, with the dream of introducing traditional Japanese humor to people all over the world. In 2019, he took part in an overseas rakugo tour and performed in front of enthusiastic audiences in the United Kingdom and Kazakhstan.

In addition to performing rakugo and serving on the Board of Directors for the English Rakugo Association in Tokyo, Koraku manages an overseas marketing company called Wasabi Communications Co., Ltd. He is also the manager of a sustainable products organization known as Camino Co., Ltd.

---

[153] Kanariya, Koraku. Email interview with the author, October 14, 2021.

KO: I understand that you ventured into the world of rakugo when you were just a high school student. When did you initially become interested in rakugo?

KK: *My parents ran a kimono business, and we always had clients visiting us from all over the country. As a small child, I was fascinated by their different accents and dialects. I couldn't help mimicking them, which made them laugh.*

I had great fun doing that, so it was natural for me to develop an interest in comedy, especially rakugo, as a tool to break the ice and make everyone happy.

KO: You gave your first rakugo performance in 1986 during a school festival. What was it like to take the stage as a rakugo storyteller for the first time? Do you remember the story you presented? Why did you choose that particular story?

KK: *I have to confess that I had an ulterior motive for performing rakugo in 1986. At that time, I had a big crush on a girl who was the leader of a rakugo club at a nearby all-girls high school. I thought that if I performed rakugo at our school festival, I would have a plausible excuse to invite her to come see me.*

On the day of the performance, all of the girls in the rakugo club, except my crush, showed up. But I enjoyed making the audience laugh so much that I didn't care whether my crush was there or not.

I performed "Jugemu," as it was pretty much a sure thing for novice rakugo performers. If you can memorize the character's ridiculously long name, a laugh is almost always guaranteed.

KO: You are quite gifted as a storyteller and have an amazing stage presence. Did the thought of becoming a professional rakugoka ever cross your mind?

KK: *Not at all! I was never good at staying in one place and doing the same thing for a long period of time. I was very active and interested in so many things. I also heard countless horror stories about the life of a rakugo apprentice. I knew I'd never last.*

But now that I'm older, I feel I'm finally ready to really learn this traditional art of storytelling.

KO: You mentioned in your English Rakugo Association bio that you became aware of the importance of mixing comedy with diplomacy while you were working in Europe and the United States. Can you elaborate on that?

How did comedy add to your success in business? What motivated you to continue your rakugo studies?

KK: *My job as a diplomat required quite a bit of public speaking at conferences as well as socializing at receptions and dinners. Although it is a well-known fact that Japanese people are not good at communicating in English, let alone telling jokes, I was constantly looking for good jokes and humorous anecdotes related to Japan or Japanese people to help break the ice and keep the audience entertained during my speeches.*

Whether it be in diplomacy or in business, a successful outcome is dependent on the trust that exists between you and your counterparts. Good communication filled with laughter is a key to building that trust.

I continue my rakugo studies because it provides me with the ideal training to be funny. I often find myself having to come up with a funny, informative, and entertaining introduction within a short span of time.

I realized a long time ago that one of the few assets I have is the fact that I look Japanese and I am Japanese. If I do something traditionally Japanese, I'd probably look authentic no matter how hopeless I may be!

When I watched my master, Eiraku, performing English rakugo on TV in 2018, I knew instantly that this was exactly what I was looking for, something that requires English speaking skills as well as "Japaneseness."

KO: When did you begin your Japanese rakugo studies with Kingetei Ryoma shisho?

If you can point out one very important thing that Ryoma shisho taught you, what would it be?

KK: *I began taking lessons from Ryoma shisho in 2018. I can't seem to recall a specific important lesson right now, but I'm thrilled to have the opportunity to see a real shinuchi perform in front of me.*

It also delights me to perform in front of him and have him provide detailed comments about what I could do better.

KO: When did you begin studying English rakugo with Kanariya Eiraku-san?

Was it easy to transition from Japanese rakugo to English rakugo? If not, what were some of the challenges?

KK: *I began to study English rakugo around the same time in 2018. I wanted to be able to tell a story in different languages, so I thought it made sense to learn it properly in Japanese first.*

However, there were a few occasions during which I was distracted, or lost my concentration, and forgot if I was speaking in Japanese or English! It usually gets very tricky after a callout or after acting out a part with no lines. Luckily, it hasn't happened when I was performing in front of the audience! Yet!

KO: Do you have a favorite rakugo performer, or one who may have influenced you as a storyteller?

KK: *Among many of my favorite performers, one that stands out is Takigawa Risho. He is a seasoned performer in his late sixties. As soon as he comes out on stage and kneels down on the zabuton, he typically broadens his trademark wide eyes and looks around at the audience with a big grin showing his protruding teeth. This immediately breaks the ice with the audience and even creates laughter before his storytelling begins.*

Contrary to his unique visual presence, his storytelling is actually very classy and sophisticated, and yet hilarious in a very decent way.

His stage presence is amazing and his storytelling skills are even more extraordinary.

KO: You seem to be a devoted linguist, and you mentioned that you would like to become Japan's first multi-lingual rakugo performer. In addition to Japanese and English, in what other languages would you like to perform rakugo?

KK: *Since childhood, I've developed something of a fetish for different languages. I've just started performing rakugo in French and I hope to try it in Italian as these are the languages I'm most familiar with.*

Speaking a different language is like living someone else's life or having another persona within you, which I find quite addictive. I'm also hoping to learn at least one story, such as "Jugemu," in German, Russian, and Spanish.

KO: You mentioned that you favor humorous stories such as "Chiritotechin" and "Complimenting a Child." Have you considered writing your own rakugo stories?

KK: *I'd love to. I was fortunate enough to have spent some time in different countries as a teenager and also as an adult. As a result, I've come across many embarrassing moments either because of the language barrier, or because of pretense, that are worth writing about. At the moment, I'm working out the plot.*

KO: You are very busy, and not only as a rakugo performer. You are also a board member of the English Rakugo Association (ERA), and you manage an overseas marketing company called Wasabi Communications Co., Ltd, and a sustainable products organization called Camino Co., Ltd.

One of the sustainable products Camino manufactures is a handheld fan. (FANO). I thought it was very interesting that a young kabuki actor named Nakamura Hashigo became the ambassador of FANO. Have you considered a sustainable sensu for rakugo performers?

KK: *Absolutely! But my staff is worried that I might donate all the profits to the ERA instead of raising their salaries, so I'm torn about what to do!*

xxii. Kanariya Simon (*Photo by Kanariya Kichiyu*)

23. KANARIYA SIMON

"I really want rakugo to come to represent Japan overseas in the same way kabuki, sumo wrestling, and manga do.

In order for this to happen, Japanese people have to accept and respect English rakugo performers."

— Kanariya Simon (August 31, 2021)[154]

In his elementary school days, Simon fell in love with and devoted himself to learning numerous Japanese rakugo stories. In April 2014, he joined the Canary English Rakugo class, with the hope of improving his English conversation skills; however, he could not set aside his love for the art of storytelling and soon began to think about introducing rakugo beyond the borders of Japan.

Wanting to expand his English rakugo repertoire, he embarked on a project in 2017 to translate various koten rakugo stories into English. To date, he has translated 10 of the 15 stories he regularly performs on stage. Translating humorous Japanese rakugo stories into English is Simon's favorite pastime.

---

[154] Kanariya, Simon. Email interview with the author, August 31, 2021.

He has a deep love for rakugo, and even his five-year-old daughter can tell whether he is going to work or to his rakugo lessons based on his mood when he leaves his house!

> KO: You mentioned that you loved rakugo even as an elementary school student. What influenced you? Did a family member introduce you to rakugo, or was it something you saw on television or heard on the radio?

> KS: *I had a chance to travel to the United States when I was eight or so. I got bored during the long flight and decided to listen to the radio. At the time, the only in-flight station available in Japanese was the rakugo station. I think that was my first encounter with rakugo and I really got into it.*

> KO: As a young boy, did you have a favorite rakugo storyteller? If so, why was this person your favorite rakugoka?

> KS: *When I was a kid, Shunputei Koasa and Tatekawa Shinosuke were my favorites. What appealed to me most about the two was that they performed rakugo in their own individual styles rather than just perpetuating the traditional style of performance they were taught.*

Later, I learned that it was something that Tatekawa Danshi initiated; he started to inject koten rakugo with modern values and sensibilities. Shinosuke is one of Danshi's finest disciples, and Koasa was someone Danshi adored even though he is not one of his disciples.

After getting to know more about Danshi, I really fell in love with his rakugo and philosophy. Shinosuke is still my favorite as well.

KO: What was the first rakugo story you learned when you began memorizing stories? Why did you choose this story?

KS: *I never consciously tried to memorize rakugo stories, actually. As a child, I repeatedly listened to the stories on CDs and I memorized them subconsciously.*

When I became interested in rakugo, I purchased several CDs featuring Shinosuke. I memorized "Tohnasuya Seidan" ("The Case of the Pumpkin Peddler"), "Senryo Mikan" ("One Thousand Ryo Tangerine"), "Okechimyaku" ("Bloodline Stamp"), and "Nezumi Ana" ("A Mouse Hole"), among others. Although each story is approximately 40 minutes long, and the words used in these stories are very difficult for a child, I memorized those stories entirely — while imitating Shinosuke's rhythm and tone.

I think that learning rakugo's rhythm and tone when I was young really helped me as an English rakugo performer.

KO: How did you learn about Kanariya Eiraku and the Canary English Rakugo class?

KS: *I was just looking for an opportunity to speak English in order to improve my speaking ability. I thought about joining an English drama club, but that requires getting together with people, of course. As I was thinking about "How I can practice speaking English anytime, anywhere, by myself," I hit upon the idea to try rakugo in English.*

I never thought I would actually find someone who teaches English using rakugo, but I tried searching the internet for an "English rakugo class" and found the Canary English Rakugo class.

After I joined, I learned that master Eiraku had been a member of Tatekawa-ryu, which my favorite rakugo performer, Tatekawa Danshi, established.

I think it was pure destiny. Now I believe I found a place where I can really devote myself.

KO: When did you begin learning English?

KS: *Like most Japanese students at that time, I started learning English in junior high school when I was 12. During that time, I enjoyed learning English by listening to English songs.*

KO: What made you want to spread rakugo outside of Japan?

KS: *It was an ambition which gradually developed inside of me.*

When I started translating the koten pieces into English, I rediscovered Japanese culture and the customs which I normally take for granted, but find it difficult to explain why they exist and why we adhere to them.

For instance, why did people in Edo move so frequently? Why was a second-hand shop called a "dohgu-ya" so popular at that time? Why was a doctor relegated to a low social standing in society? These are interesting topics even for the

Japanese, and I thought foreigners may be just as interested in learning about our culture.

In February 2018, I participated in the Arizona Matsuri in Phoenix, where I performed English rakugo. That was my first experience performing rakugo in front of a large foreign audience. After seeing many foreigners laughing at my story, I realized that rakugo can be understood and enjoyed by foreigners too.

After that, a gentleman who works as a tour guide joined the Canary English Rakugo class. Although he left soon thereafter, I was really impressed with his passion for wanting to spread Japanese culture all over the world. While talking with him, as one rakugo lover who can speak English to another, I felt that I had a duty to spread Japanese culture through rakugo.

Now, whenever I translate rakugo into English, I am translating with a foreign audience in mind. I feel the burden of the need to translate rakugo and perform it well because if I don't, people will presume rakugo is boring — and that is something I cannot accept.

KO: How do you select which stories to translate?

KS: *Basically, I translate my favorite stories one by one. I always have several candidates to consider, and I determine the order in which I want to translate each one.*

There are some very important points in selecting a story. First, you have to ask yourself whether the punchline can easily be understood. This is the minimum requirement.

Many of the Japanese punchlines cannot be translated directly into English and they need to be changed and presented in another way. If I cannot come up with a good punchline in English, I won't pick that story regardless of how much I love it. I still have a huge backlog of stories I want to translate, but finding a good punchline is important.

Second, does the story convey something about Japanese culture, customs, feelings that I want to introduce to the world? My purpose for performing English rakugo is to introduce foreigners to Japanese culture, so this is also mandatory.

Third, can I make the stories more interesting by adding my own ideas, jokes, phrases? This is something I want to strive for, and if I can satisfy this criterion also, that story will most likely become my favorite script.

KO: What are some of the challenges you face when you are translating stories and how do you overcome these challenges?

KS: *The biggest challenge is to create a meaningful and interesting story in English with a great punchline. It may sound like a contradiction that I want to spread Japanese culture to the world through English rakugo.*

I personally think that English rakugo cannot be compared to Japanese rakugo. English rakugo was born from Japanese rakugo, of course, but they are two different things to me. Some people say English rakugo cannot surpass the original rakugo, and even I felt that way before, but now I think that you cannot compare the two because they are two different things like baseball and softball, or football and futsal. It always starts from the original Japanese story, but what I am doing is reconstructing a different dialogue in English.

I have several methods for reconstructing dialogue. One is to pick up some key words from the original Japanese story and look for English idioms using those key words. These could become the punchline in the English version.

Another technique is to intentionally add some Japanese words which are familiar to foreigners, like ninja, geisha etc., even when they don't appear in the original story. I think that makes audiences feel that the story is more interesting and exotic.

On the other hand, I sometimes introduce Western culture or a Western character in my story. In one of my koten rakugo scripts, Pinocchio appears! This culture gap makes it funny and it is something we can only do in English rakugo.

KO: What is your vision for the future of rakugo? What do you want to see happen?

KS: *I really want rakugo to come to represent Japan overseas in the same way kabuki, sumo wrestling, and manga do. In order for this to happen, Japanese people have to accept and respect English rakugo performers.*

For this reason, I will keep performing and translating koten rakugo pieces into English.

KO: Has your daughter watched your rakugo performances? What does she think about her father performing rakugo?

KS: *She has seen my performances online only one or two times. Although she cannot understand English, she seemed to enjoy my performance, sitting on a zabuton, wearing a kimono, and portraying various characters.*

She recently became interested in Japanese rakugo and began memorizing some phrases from stories like "Jugemu." She also wants to learn English now and come see me perform in the theater.

xxiii. Kanariya Usagi (*Photo by Kanariya Kichiyu*)

24. KANARIYA USAGI

"If the performer cannot enjoy performing the story, how can the audience enjoy the story?"

— Kanariya Usagi [155]

Kanariya Usagi began studying English rakugo in 2009 in an effort to entertain foreign tourists, but she soon became captivated by the more subtle aspects of rakugo storytelling. Today, she not only performs English rakugo, but she also translates koten rakugo stories into English.

She has taken her rakugo performances from the tour bus to foreign countries and seeks to introduce the art form and Japanese culture in general to English-speaking audiences worldwide someday.

KO: You began studying English rakugo in 2009. What was your motivation to study rakugo and why did you choose English rakugo?

KU: When I began studying English rakugo in 2009, I never imagined that I would be able to continue doing it for such a long time. What prompted me to study rakugo in the first

---

[155] Kanariya, Usagi. Email interview with the author, September 29, 2021.

place was my job. I have been working as a tour guide for foreign tourists since 2006. My job involves entertaining customers. In fact, it is part and parcel of the job. I'm always thinking about how to make them happy.

One day at a bookshop, I came across an English rakugo book with a CD. I purchased it and listened to it at home. It was so funny that I could not stop laughing. I was amazed to learn that rakugo, which is a traditional Japanese art form, was interesting enough to make people laugh, even in English. I realized then that this was exactly what I was looking for. But I had no idea how to pursue it.

I talked about my interest in English rakugo with a friend of mine and he found an English rakugo school, whose name was Canary Rakugo School. This is how I encountered English rakugo.

KO: When did you first become interested in rakugo as an art form?

KU: *It is hard to say when I became aware of rakugo as an art form. At first it was only an entertainment tool for my customers. But I soon became hooked on the more subtle aspects of rakugo storytelling.*

Rakugo is the simple art of storytelling. Anyone can perform it, if only if they can memorize a story. While it looks easy, it actually requires certain skills such as using a deliberate pitch of voice and eloquent facial expressions. The storyteller must also be capable of executing elaborate poses between lines. Rakugo is simple, but complex.

This deceptive simplicity interested me, and before realizing it, I was already deeply involved in rakugo.

Rakugo has survived for 400 years as a traditional Japanese art form. There are probably many reasons why it has endured so long — although I don't know what they are exactly. But I'm sure there is something about rakugo which attracts people.

KO: Your stage name Usagi is rather cute! How did you come up with it?

KU: *Usagi means rabbit in English. Rabbits get lonely easily, but they don't like being with many other rabbits. I'm a lonely person, but I get stressed in a crowd. I am like a rabbit in that regard. That's why I chose this stage name.*

Everyone says Usagi is the perfect stage name for me. Rabbits are cute enough to soothe us. I am happy if my companions feel comfortable when they are with me.

KO: You mentioned that you became interested in rakugo because of the line of work you are in. How do you use rakugo as a bus tour guide?

KU: *There is a term, "Ichigo Ichie." It literally means a once-in-a lifetime encounter. This expression comes from the tea ceremony.*

The idea is that each occasion is very special and never repeatable. Therefore, the host must try to do their best to entertain the guests. This is my job philosophy.

I want my customers, who may visit Japan only once in their lifetime, to take home a lot of good memories of Japan. This motivated me to present rakugo or short comic stories in front of my tour members.

Our tour bus sometimes gets stuck in traffic jams, and rather than risk a bus full of sighs and yawns, I present rakugo to reduce stress. When people laugh, they feel happy. When my customers are happy, I'm happy. In other words, rakugo makes everyone on the bus happy.

I had one unforgettable encounter several years ago. I presented a short comic story on the bus. A teenager came up to me afterwards and said that he knew the story because his father had told it to him after returning from Japan. His father joined my tour group the year before. I was delighted to hear that because his father had taken the story back home as a pleasant memory. That young man told me that I was the funniest guide he had ever met. It was the best compliment I have ever received.

KO: You have travelled to the United States and Laos to perform. How would you describe your experiences performing rakugo in front of foreign audiences?

KU: *Performing rakugo overseas was a precious experience for me. It is quite something. Not many people can do it. I think performing rakugo in front of foreign audiences has both its advantages and disadvantages.*

One advantage is that since the foreign audience's reaction is quick and open, it gets me going. They laugh if they think it is funny. Laughter is contagious. One person's laughter draws laughter from others to create more laughter. It helps pump me up and contributes to a good performance. This is the biggest advantage.

The disadvantage is that since a lot of foreign audiences are unfamiliar with Japanese culture, I need to explain the things unique to Japan such as traditional customs and specific ways to conduct ceremonies. However, a lengthy explanation will ruin a well-designed story. So, I need to describe naturally what these things are either with my acting or with the narrative.

This is what I realized by performing rakugo in front of foreign audiences.

KO: If given the opportunity to tour overseas again, would you do it? What countries would you like to perform in, and why?

KU: *Yes, I'd love to join the overseas tours again. I don't have any particular country in mind. Any country is OK with me if it is safe and people there understand English. I will be very proud to introduce rakugo to people in other cultures.*

KO: Rakugo was once a male-dominated art form, and consequently suitable stories for female rakugoka to perform are somewhat limited. What stories do you enjoy performing? What stories would you like to learn and perform in the future?

KU: *Most rakugo stories were created by men from a man's point of view, and some included dirty jokes. Female rakugo performers, myself included, probably would not feel comfortable performing such stories. In this sense, my options for suitable stories to perform will be limited to some extent.*

While most stories are from the man's perspective, I choose the stories that show the tender side of the Japanese. For example, I like stories that show the husband is bossy in appearance, but actually he is henpecked and controlled by his wife, yet they have a good relationship. In rakugo, these types of stories are very common even though this type of family is quickly fading away.

A good example is "Kawarime" ("Another Bottle of Sake"). In the story, a drunken husband asks his wife for more sake. When she turns him down, he starts complaining about her attitude. She offers sake to him against her better judgement and then her husband orders her to serve him some food with the sake. The wife goes out to buy food. He begins talking to himself in her absence about how much he loves her and how grateful he is to her. Then he notices his wife is still at the door smiling.

The characters in this story are typical Japanese in old Japan who tend to hide their true feelings in the presence of people. I love this story. Their conversations are full of humor and love. Rakugo stories provide insights into people in old Japan. I'd like to perform stories which include that essence.

KO: I understand that you have been translating rakugo stories into English since 2015. What motivated you to do this?

KU: *Back in 2015, I began translating rakugo stories into English; however, before then I had translated some short comic stories for my tour members. I was happy and amazed to realize my translations made them laugh. This became my motivation to start translating rakugo stories.*

I like both performing and translating rakugo. But if I had to choose, I'd say I prefer translating. This is probably attributable to the fact that I'm shy.

But my translated works are like my children. They make their debut when I perform them. I'm responsible for sending my children out into the world. That is why I appear on the stage.

KO: Which stories have you translated so far? Why did you choose those particular stories?

KU: *I have translated nine stories so far, including "Uranai yaoya" ("Fortunetelling Grocer"), "Bakemonozukai" ("Monster Slave Driver"), and "Horinouchi" ("Myouhouji Temple"). I chose these stories because they are funny and I like to see people laughing.*

There are some requirements for selecting which stories I will translate. First, it should be a story I want to perform. If the performer cannot enjoy performing the story, how can the audience enjoy the story?

Second, the story must be simple enough to be understood by the foreign audience who is not familiar with Japanese culture. A lot of explanation will spoil the story.

Third, the story must be as interesting in English as it is in the original Japanese. I choose the stories based on these requirements, and I would like to continue translating the stories that can entertain both the performer and the audience.

KO: Would you encourage other women to join the world of rakugo?

KU: *Yes, I would. If we have more female rakugoka, stories created by women would increase. Most rakugo stories today were produced by men. I would like to listen to stories created from a woman's point of view. It would excite me.*

If women who are interested in rakugo feel it is difficult to join the rakugo world as performers, I think they should join as audience members. The rakugo world was once a man's world and most audience members were men. However, these days, women audience members outnumber men during rakugo recitals. Maybe this is partly because there are more female rakugoka now. I'd be happy to see more women join the rakugo world to make it popular.

KO: What appeals to you about the rakugo world?

KU: *I'd say it is the deceptive simplicity of rakugo. It looks easy, but actually it's very difficult to perform well. I still have a long way to go to become a good performer. However, someday I'd like to mesmerize people with my storytelling. Such motivation attracts me to rakugo.*

In addition, many of the people I have met in the rakugo world appeal to me. They are my charming companions. They are the people with a good sense of humor, like the characters in the rakugo stories. We have inspired each other and improved our skills. I can be myself around them.

The Scripts

The koten rakugo scripts presented here were translated and performed by **Kanariya Eiraku** *to English-speaking audiences in Japan and overseas.*

xxiv. Big Sale (*By Kei Ohsuga*)

Translation:

Wrestler: *"The next name for me will be Big Sale!"*

Man: *"Big Sale?"*

Big Sale (*Oh-Yasuuri*)

Characters:

S: Sumo wrestler
A, B: Townspeople

There are several rakugo stories about sumo wrestlers, including "Hanaikada," "Sanoyama," "Ohnomatsu," "Inagawa," "Kuwagawa," and "Oh-Yasuuri." All the story titles are the names of sumo wrestlers, real or fictitious.

The following is the story of "Big Sale," or "Oh-Yasuuri."

A: Hey, look over there.
B: Where?
A: There. There's a man walking toward us.
B: Yes, he is big. Who is he?
A: He is a sumo wrestler.
    The other day, when I visited Mr. Iwata, a retired old man, he introduced me to that guy.
    Hello, mister!
S: Hello, you work as a carpenter in this town, don't you?
A: Yes, I do.

	I haven't seen you for a while.
S:	I went to Osaka with my master.
	I am still a beginner, but thanks to my master and my supporters, I was able to participate in the sumo tournament there.
A:	That's great!
	You show respect for your seniors.
	The world of sumo is extremely hierarchical.
	First you have to thank your master and your supporters.
	I appreciate your attitude.
	How did you do in your matches?
S:	I did my best for ten days.
	There were some wins and there were some losses.
A:	Great!
	Usually those who go to Osaka say they won all the matches.
	Osaka is hundreds of miles away from here, so there is no way to confirm the results.
	If they say they won, we believe them and tip them.
	But you are different.
	You said there were some wins and there were some losses.
	You are very honest.
	I like an honest man like you.

	I will support you.
	How was your sumo on the first day?
S:	I was tense on the first day.
	I dashed toward my opponent, but he slapped me down to the ring.
A:	I see.
	So you lost the match on the first day.
	I don't blame you for being nervous.
	After all, you are a beginner and it's the first time for you to join the sumo tournament in Osaka.
	How about the second day?
S:	I knew I could not afford to lose.
	If I lost, I couldn't face my master and all my supporters.
	So I dashed toward my opponent, grabbed his belt, and pushed him toward the edge of the ring!
A:	There you go!
	That must be your favorite technique.
	So you won!
S:	No, he caught my belt and pivoted to throw me out of the ring at the last minute.
A:	Oh, so you lost.
	How about the third day?
S:	I knew I could not afford to lose again.

	If I lost, I couldn't face my master and all my supporters.
	So I dashed toward my opponent and tried to slap him down.
A:	Sounds great!
	That must be another favorite technique of yours.
	Did he fall down to the ground?
S:	When I tried to slap his face, he ducked his head down.
	So I could not slap him.
	Then he kicked my leg and I fell down.
A:	Is that so?
	You were unlucky.
	So you lost again.
	How about the fourth day?
S:	I knew I could not afford to lose again.
	If I lost, I couldn't face my master and all my supporters.
	So I dashed toward the opponent and tried to hold his leg with my hands.
A:	Wow, you did something your opponent did not expect you to do!
	What happened?
	Did it work?

S: He quickly stepped backward so I could not hold his leg.
A: I see.
He reacted very quickly to your trick.
What did you do after that?
S: I dashed toward him, but I could not stop, so I just ran out of the ring.
A: Oh, my!
So you lost again.
How about the fifth day?
S: I knew I could not afford to lose again. If I lost…
A: Wait! That's enough.
You don't have to thank your master or your supporters any more.
I got tired of it.
Just tell me what happened in the ring?
S: I see. My opponent on the fifth day was injured.
He had bandages on his elbows, knees, wrists, and ankles.
I did not want to fight such a wrestler, but I thought it would be poor sportsmanship if I did not fight with all my might.
A: Yes, you are right!
That's professionalism.
You always have to do your best.

	Otherwise, you will dishonor him.
	How did you fight him?
S:	I tried to kick his knees wrapped in bandages.
A:	What! You kicked his knees wrapped in bandages?
	That's not fair!
	That's poor sportsmanship.
	Do you want to win like that?
S:	I did not win.
	My kick did not reach his knee and I slipped and touched the ground.
A:	What?
	You couldn't even defeat an injured man like him?
	How about the sixth day?
S:	On the sixth day, I tried to push my opponent over by catching his ankle with my leg from inside.
A:	Ah, that's known as the "inside leg trip."
	I know the technique!
S:	Then, he pushed me over by catching my ankle with his leg from outside.
A:	Ah, that's known as the "outside leg trip," I know that technique as well.
	That means he did it first and it looked like an inside leg trip to you.
	You just didn't do anything.
	How about the seventh day?

S: On the seventh day, I tried to slap my opponent's face.

A: That's your favorite; slapping faces.
Did it work this time?

S: My fingers went into his eyes by mistake.
I didn't do it intentionally, but that was forbidden.
I lost the match on account of a foul.

A: I see.
You were unlucky.
How about the eighth day?

S: On the eighth day, my opponent used a mean technique!

A: Is that so?
I hear sumo wrestlers in Osaka sometimes use dirty tricks.
What did he do?

S: He grabbed my belt, lifted me up and took me out of the ring.

A: That's called a "lift out." There's nothing wrong with it.

S: Is that so?
Is that a regular technique?
I didn't know.

A: Are you really a sumo wrestler?
I can't believe it.

	You should be ashamed of yourself.
	What about the ninth day?
S:	My opponent was over six feet tall and weighed over 400 pounds.
A:	Wow, I've never seen such a big wrestler in Tokyo.
	It is difficult to beat such a huge guy.
	What did you do?
S:	I sat on the ring and apologized to him.
A:	What?
	You gave up fighting him?
	What a poor wrestler you are!
	How about the tenth day, the final day?
S:	I was sick.
	So I did not join the sumo tournament.
	I lost by default.
A:	Gosh. You defaulted.
	That means you lost all ten matches.
	But you said in the beginning that there were wins and losses.
S:	Yes, wins on the opponent side and losses on my side.
A:	Oh, that's what you meant.
	Did you return to Tokyo after that?
S:	No, I stopped off in Nagoya on the way back to Tokyo.
	I had no losses in Nagoya.

A: I see.

You know how to tell a story.

First you talk about your losses and next you talk about your wins.

Tell me more about it.

S: I got infected by a new virus, so I was sick in bed during the tournament.

A: What?

You got infected with a virus?

Weren't you vaccinated?

S: I was fully vaccinated, but still I got infected.

You need to be careful.

A: I see.

So you were in bed all through the tournament.

You had no losses simply because you didn't fight.

Did you return to Tokyo after you were cured?

S: No, I visited Shizuoka, where I fought amateur sumo wrestlers and I had five straight wins!

A: You finally won!

That's what I wanted to hear.

Five straight wins.

That's incredible.

Congratulations!

S: Don't praise me.

They are amateurs, after all.

A: You deserve to be complimented.

Amateurs these days are very strong.

Some are even as strong as the pros.

What did the first opponent look like?

S: He was a six-year-old boy.

A: What!

Was he only six years old?

I can beat him too!

I hope you didn't injure him.

You'd better think about your career.

Are you going to continue sumo?

S: I was debating whether I should continue or not and talked with my master.

He advised me to continue.

A: Is that right?

That means your master thinks you're going to be a good wrestler.

What did he say?

S: He said if I quit, there would be no one to walk his dog.

A: What!

Is that the reason he didn't want you to quit?

You should reconsider your future.

S: Yes, I'm thinking about changing my ring name and starting all over again.

A: That is a good idea.

There have been some wrestlers who grew stronger after changing their ring name.

What will your new name be?

S: Big Sale.

A: Big Sale?

That's an unusual name.

Usually, sumo wrestlers' names include a letter which represents a mountain, a sea, a river, or a valley because it makes the wrestler sound strong.

Why did you choose the name Big Sale?

S: With that name, my opponents will discount my skill.

xxv. Bloodline Stamp (*By Kei Ohsuga*)

Translation:

Demon: *"Mr. Ishikawa, Mr. Ishikawa!"*

Goemon: *"What do you want?"*

Bloodline Stamp (*Okechimyaku*)

Characters:

K:	Enma (The King of Hell)
S:	Enma's servant
I:	Ishikawa Goemon, a thief
M:	A man
B:	A Buddha statue

Buddhism is a lenient religion because Buddhists believe that everyone can go to heaven. Even a sinful man would be permitted to go to heaven.

In Shinshu, (now known as Nagano), there is a very old temple called Zenkoji. It derives its name from a particular man.

One day, when this man was walking along a pond in Nara, he heard someone call out his name. When he turned around, he saw that it was a small statue of Buddha speaking to him. He bowed to the Buddha statue.

M: Yes, what can I do for you?

B: I'd like to go to Shinshu. Can you take me there?

The man agreed and he walked all the way from Nara to Shinshu to deliver the statue of Buddha to the temple, where it was later enshrined. That was how Zenkoji Temple originated. It was built in 644 when Buddhism was not yet divided into many sects.

In time, the temple provided a means for people to ascend to Heaven. If they donated some money to the temple, the monk prayed and stamped their forehead with a bloodline stamp or an okechimyaku. It was believed that by receiving the stamp, a person's bloodline would be connected to the bloodline of Buddha, allowing the person to gain immediate entrance to Heaven. Therefore, it was called the bloodline stamp or okechimyaku.

Soon, word spread all over Japan and everybody donated to the temple and went to Heaven. Consequently, Hell was economically devastated. Enma, the king of Hell, sold some of his belongings to help support Hell's economy. Two of his trusted aids, the Red Demon and the Blue Demon, grew malnourished and their color faded. They sold all their spare underwear, so they wore the same underwear every day and began to stink. To address this situation, they decided to have an emergency meeting presided over by Enma.

K: Ladies and gentlemen, thank you for attending this urgent meeting. As you know, we are facing a serious financial problem. We must tackle this situation right away. Does anyone have any ideas?

S: Your majesty, can I say a few words?

K: Yes, go ahead.

S: Why not steal the stamp from the temple so that people can no longer go to Heaven and will be sent to Hell instead?

K: What a great idea! And who can we entrust with this important task?

S: This is Hell. We have a lot of thieves here.

K: Then look at the list of thieves and tell me, who is the best qualified?

S: How about Rat Boy?

K: Hmm, Rat Boy. He is a good pickpocket, but we can't send a boy to do a man's job.

S: Then how about Ms. Omasa, the Viper?

K: Ms. Omasa, the Viper? She is good, but we can't send a woman to do a man's job either.

S: Then what about Arsene Lupin?

K: Lupin is French. I didn't know he was here. But he doesn't speak Japanese. We can't send a foreign thief to do this job.

S: Then why not ask Ishikawa Goemon?

K: Ishikawa Goemon! Yes, he is perfect for this mission. What's he doing now?

S: He is taking a hot bath. It was supposed to be his punishment, but now he got used to the heat and he is

K: enjoying a hot bath. He is practicing kabuki while soaking in the bathtub. He loves kabuki.
K: I see. He is an interesting guy. Send for him right away.

The King's servant immediately went to fetch Ishikawa Goemon.

S: Mr. Ishikawa, Mr. Ishikawa!
I: Yes, you are the King's servant. What can I do for you?
S: The King wants to see you.
I: What does he want me to do?
S: I don't know. But I heard that he wants to send you back to the real world. If you do a good job, you can become an executive in Hell.
I: Really? That sounds good.
S: Please hurry. The King is waiting for you.
I: Wait a second. Get me that costume!
S: OK. Oh, this is the costume you wore when you performed a kabuki play during the cherry blossom viewing festival.
I: Yes, that's right. I wear this costume when I am asked to go on an important mission.
S: I see. Let's go.

Goemon wore a gorgeous kimono with a flashy sash, a fashionable haori jacket, and a pair of expensive shoes before he set out to meet the King.

I: Your majesty, here I am. I'm Ishikawa Goemon.

K: Glad to meet you, Mr. Ishikawa. Come closer.

I: It is embarrassing for me to come closer to the King.

K: No, no, you just make yourself at home. As you may have heard, we are facing a serious financial problem because Zenkoji Temple in the real world possesses what they call a bloodline stamp. When a person is stamped on the forehead with this stamp, he will immediately go to Heaven. So, I would like for you to steal the stamp from the temple. Are you willing to accept this mission?

I: I was wondering what kind of favor you would ask of me. Stealing a stamp from a temple is a piece of cake. When I was in the real world, I learned all the skills of a Ninja.

I made some mistakes when I entered the estate of Lord Toyotomi Hideyoshi. As a result, I was captured and sentenced to death. Now that you have entrusted me with this important task, I will never repeat the mistakes I made earlier, and I will complete this job. You don't have to worry about a thing.

K: That's good! Now hurry up and go to the temple.

I: Yes, sir.

Goemon answered in the grand kabuki style and left.

During the day, he searched the temple buildings. At night, he entered the temple sanctuary using his Ninja skills. He investigated every jewelry box and eventually found a wooden box with a tag which read bloodline stamp. He opened the box only to find another box, and then another box. Finally, he found the stamp wrapped in a cotton cloth. Now that he had the stamp, all he had to do was to take it to the King of Hell. But he could not resist performing kabuki before departing the temple.

I: I successfully sneaked into the sanctuary of Zenkoji Temple and found the bloodline stamp. I stole it and completed my mission. Thank you very much, Buddha!

He placed the stamp on his forehead and he went straight to Heaven.

xxvi. Complimenting a Child (*By Kei Ohsuga*)

Translation:

Hachi: *"Yes, he is big!"*

Complimenting a Child (*Kohome*)

Characters:

H:	Hachi
I:	Inkyo
HAN:	Hanji
T:	Take

In Japan's bygone days, when a child was born, it was already considered one year old. In those days, everyone grew one year older on New Year's Day instead of on the day they were actually born. There wasn't much talk about birthdays back then. The New Year holiday was much more important for the Japanese than their own birthday.

H:	Hello, Inkyo.
I:	Hello, Hachi, how are you?
H:	Fine, thank you.
	I heard you have some good sake. Is that true?
I:	Yes, my relative gave me some good sake yesterday.
H:	Can I have some of it for nothing?
I:	For nothing?
H:	Yes, for nothing. For free.
	Why don't you treat me?

I: If you want to have something for nothing, you should pay a compliment.

H: What's a compliment?

I: A compliment is a phrase that makes people happy.

H: Is it difficult?

I: No, it isn't. It's easy.

When you meet someone on the street, what do you say?

H: Well, I say, "What's up, you bastard?"

I: Oh, you should watch your language!

You should be more polite.

You should say, "Good day, sir. It's been a long time since we last met. I heard your business has been good, and your children are doing very well in school."

H: Oh, I see. So, a compliment means telling a lie.

I: Well, sort of.

But if you pay such a compliment, you might be treated to a few drinks.

H: Sounds good.

But if he doesn't treat me, then what can I do?

I: In that case, you ask his age.

"How old are you?" you ask. He'll say, "I'm 50."

Then you say, "Oh you look much younger. I thought you are 45 or 46."

	Then he'll be happy, and he will say, "You are a nice guy. Let's go and have a few drinks. I'll treat you."
H:	That's great! Compliments are convenient.
	But I have a question. Not everyone is 50. What if he is 60 years old?
I:	It's easy. You should say 55 or 56.
H:	How about 70?
I:	You should say 65 or 66.
H:	How about 80?
I:	The same as before.
H:	I see. So when I meet a person of 80, I say, "the same as before."
I:	No, no. That's not what I meant.
	You should say 75 or 76.
H:	How about 90?
I:	You should say 85 or 86.
H:	How about 100?
I:	Hey, how many 100-year-olds are walking around these days? But if there were, you should say 95 or 96.
H:	How about 1,000?
I:	Stop it! People like Frankenstein and Dracula do not exist!
H:	It's a big world, there could be such a person somewhere. I have to be prepared. Can I say 995 or 996?

I: OK, OK! That's enough.

The point is you should subtract a few years from his real age.

That way your compliment cannot fail.

H: Great! So, when I meet a father and child, I ask the father, "How old is your son?"

He says, "He is 9."

Then I say, "Oh your son looks much younger than that. I thought he was 6."

Does that work?

I: No. With children and teenagers, you should use the opposite rule.

If he says, "He is 9," you should say, "He looks far more intelligent and mature than that. I thought he was 12."

Then his father will be very happy.

He will say, "You are a nice guy. It's lunchtime. Do you want to join us?"

How is that?

H: Great! A compliment can lead not only to drinks, but also food. If I master the compliment, I can live without money, huh?

I: That may be possible.

The point is you add 3 to the real age.

H: How about a baby?

"Oh, he is two."

"Oh, he looks much older, I thought he was five."

Is that OK?

I: No, it's not.

With babies there are some conventional phrases. Listen. "Is this your baby? I've never seen such a cute baby in my life! In his face, I can see that he will have a long life, just like his grandfather who died last year."

There is a proverb which says, "A chinaberry is fragrant even as a sprout."

It means, "Genius displays itself even in childhood."

"Having such a good baby is a delight. I hope I will be just as lucky when I have a child of my own."

H: Oh, the compliment is getting complicated.

Anyway, thank you for your advice.

Good-bye.

(*Walking.*)

This is a good idea. I'd like to try the compliment.

Oh, there is my friend Hanji.

Hanji, how are you?

HAN: Hey, the most handsome guy in town!

H: Wow, he is so good at giving compliments. I have to treat him.

OK, I'll make you happy.

It's been a long time since we last met.

HAN: I met you at a public bath last night.

H: Ah, that's right. It's been a long time since then.

HAN: I met you at a cigarette shop this morning.

H: Oh, yes.

Ah, where have you been?

You must have been busy, right?

HAN: No, I haven't gone anywhere.

And like you, I am not very busy.

H: I see. By the way, how old are you?

HAN: What? You know how old I am.

I'm the same age as you are. I'm 40.

H: Forty? I was not told what to say to a man of 40.

Should I say he looks younger or older?

Can you change your age to 45?

HAN: What!

H: Pleeease….

HAN: No, I don't want to.

H: You are my best friend.

HAN: What are you up to?

You are acting so strangely today.

OK, OK, as you wish.

H: How old are you?

HAN: I'm 45.

H: Great, you look much younger.

HAN: Of course, I am 40.

H:	No, no. Stay 45. OK?
	Ask me, "How old do you think I am?"
HAN:	How old do you think I am?
H:	I think you are 42. Are you happy?
HAN:	No, I'm two years younger than that, you fool!
	(*He punches Hachi.*)
H:	Ouch! He's gone.
	Why did he get so upset?
	Now I will try complimenting a child.
	Last week, my friend Take and his wife had a baby.
	My wife gave them some money for the child.
	(*Walking.*)
	Hello, Take-san.
T:	Hi, Hachi, what's up?
H:	Well, I'm here to praise your baby.
T:	Thanks, please come in. Make yourself at home.
H:	Thank you.
	Let me see your baby.
	I paid an admission.
T:	What do you mean by that?
	My house is not a zoo.
H:	Where is your baby?
T:	There, right in front of you.
H:	Wow, how big! Huge!
T:	Yeah, even the midwife said he is big.

H:	But he has no teeth and no hair.
T:	Of course, a baby doesn't have teeth or hair.
H:	He has wrinkles.
T:	What? That is his grandpa taking a nap.
H:	His grandpa? What a scatterbrain!
T:	No, he isn't. It is you who are a scatterbrain.
	My baby is right next to grandpa.
H:	This! How small! Will he grow up?
T:	Yes, he will.
H:	His face is very red. Did you boil him?
T:	No, he is not an octopus.
H:	Look, he has cute hands. Like maple leaves.
T:	Oh, finally you said something good.
H:	But with those small hands he took my five yen.
T:	Oh, come on. Should I give it back to you?
H:	I'm just kidding. Don't get upset. He is like a doll.
T:	Thank you.
	Everyone says he looks like a monkey.
	You are the only person who said something nice.
H:	He is like a doll.
	Every time I press his stomach, it goes squeak, squeak.
T:	Stop it! Are you trying to kill my baby?
H:	Now I'll do my best to drink sake for nothing.
	I'll come up with a special phrase. That will make you happy.

	Well, Take, is this your baby?
T:	Hey, don't make me anxious.
	I'll be less confident.
	I think he is my baby.
H:	In his face, I can see that he will have a long life just like his grandfather who died last year
T:	Grandpa is taking a nap right there.
H:	Oh, yeah. What about grandma?
T:	Grandma went out to get groceries.
H:	Is that right? They are both alive!
T:	Is something wrong with that?
H:	There is a proverb which says, "A chinaberry tastes good when cooked with a bean sprout."
	I have never eaten such a baby.
	Hanging such a baby is a delight.
T:	What are you talking about?
H:	Oh, I got all mixed up.
	OK, a final question.
	How old is your baby?
T:	He was born only last week.
H:	He looks much younger than that.
T:	What do you mean? How can he be much younger?
H:	He appears to be "nothing."

Hamlet (*Hamuretto*)

Characters:

H:	Hamlet, Prince of Denmark
KH:	King Hamlet, the Ghost
Q:	The Queen
KC:	King Claudius, King Hamlet's brother
HO:	Horatio, Prince Hamlet's close friend
P:	Polonius, Employed by the King
L:	Laertes, Polonius's son

Hamlet was the prince of Denmark. He was once a cheerful young man, who after losing his father, was overcome by great sorrow. His father, King Hamlet, had passed away unexpectedly. Following the King's death, his older brother Claudius married the Queen and took over the throne. Claudius was a wicked man and Hamlet truly disliked him.

One day, a strange story reached Hamlet's ears. For three nights, the soldiers who guarded the castle had witnessed a ghost. Hamlet's best friend, Horatio, had seen the ghost too.

HO: I saw the ghost at midnight, he appeared near the castle's battlements.

He looked just like your father.

	He seemed as though he wanted to say something, but when I spoke to him, he made no answer.
	He probably wants to talk to you.
H:	Is he really my father's ghost?
HO:	I believe so.
	If you have any doubts, you should come with me tomorrow night.

The next night, Hamlet and Horatio went to the battlements where the ghost had appeared earlier.

HO:	(*Pointing to the ghost.*)
	Look, my Lord!
	Look, he comes!
KH:	My son, Hamlet!
H:	Oh, don't surprise me.
KH:	I'm sorry.
	How have you been?
H:	Good.
	Are you the ghost of my father?
KH:	Yes, I am the ghost of King Hamlet, your father.
	I must speak with you.
	Please leave your friend and come with me.
H:	I see.
	Horatio, please wait here.

I'll be back soon.

(*He follows his father.*)

Father, you don't have any legs.

Did your brother Claudius cut them off?

KH: No, I was killed by Claudius but he did not cut off my legs.

H: Then why don't you have any legs?

KH: You know I loved beer when I was alive.

After I died, I traveled around the world to sample many kinds of beer. I found Japanese beer to be the best.

As I was drinking beer in Japan, I was invited to join the Association of Japanese Ghosts.

I accepted and became a member.

Japanese ghosts are supposed to appear without legs.

H: I see.

And you also have to place your arms in front of you.

KH: You're right.

H: Tell me father, how did he kill you?

KH: That's what I wanted to talk to you about.

He poured poison into my ears while I was sleeping in the garden.

It is your duty to avenge your father.

Your mother knows how Claudius killed me, but please do not kill her.

	She will be punished by her own conscience.
	Remember what I said.
	I'll see you again.
	Now get back to your friend.
H:	I understand.
	Good-bye.
	(*Going back to Horatio.*)
	Horatio, sorry to have kept you waiting.
	The ghost was my father.
	But please say nothing about what happened tonight.
HO:	I understand.

Hamlet wanted to believe what the ghost said, but he had no proof.

H:	To be or not to be, that is the question.
	Should I put up with all the troubles, or fight against them?
	(*Pause.*)
	Yes, I have to find the truth — whether King Claudius and the Queen really planned the murder.

At that time, there came to the court a group of actors. Hamlet had seen their play before. In the play, the king was killed by his brother. Hamlet made some changes to the script and let the actors perform the play before Claudius and his wife. If they were guilty, their faces would show it.

The next evening, he invited them to watch the play. He asked Horatio to watch them closely during the play.

The play began. When the king in the play was poisoned in the garden, Claudius turned pale. He was unable to watch the rest of the play. He stood up and left with the Queen.

Q: Hamlet, you have hurt your father very much.
H: No, mother, it is you who have hurt my father.
You should confess your guilt.
(*Grabbing her by the neck.*)
Sit down here!
Q: What are you doing?
Are you going to kill me?
Help, somebody, help!
P: (*Talking behind the curtain.*)
Help, help the queen!
H: What's that?
Where does that voice come from?
From behind the curtain?

Hamlet thought that King Claudius was hiding behind the curtain. He thrust his sword through the curtain and killed him. It was not Claudius, but poor old Polonius, who was working for him.

Q: What a bloody deed this is!

H: Yes, it was a bloody deed, but it is better than to kill my father and marry his brother.

Q: (*Weeping.*)

Please forgive me.

H: Never!

KH: (*The king's ghost appears.*)

My son, Hamlet!

H: Oh, it's you again.

Don't surprise me!

KH: Oh, I'm sorry.

Don't worry.

It is only you who can see me.

I'm invisible to your mother.

Leave your mother and remember the revenge you promised.

H: I understand.

(*To his mother.*)

Mother, don't tell King Claudius that I know of his crime.

	Tell him that your son is crazy and knows nothing of his father.
Q:	I understand.

Meanwhile King Claudius was planning to kill Hamlet, for he realized how dangerous he was. The Queen told the King how Polonius was killed by Hamlet.

KC:	There is no doubt that Hamlet is crazy.
	He must be killed.
	But how?
	(*Pause.*)
	Yes, I have come up with a good plan.
	Laertes, the son of Polonius, must want to take revenge on Hamlet.
	I hear both Hamlet and Laertes are skillful fencers.
	I'll ask Laertes to have a fencing duel with Hamlet.
KC:	Laertes, come forth.
	Your father was killed by Hamlet.
	You want to avenge your father, right?
	Kill him in the fencing match.
	I'll tell Hamlet that it's only a friendly match.
	But you can kill him. Understood?

The day of the fencing duel arrived. It was held in court.

KC: All right, you two.

Let's get started.

Remember.

This is a friendly match.

Are you ready? Go!

L: Oh, Hamlet, you're so strong.

H: So are you, Laertes.

I've never fought such a skillful fencer like you before.

KC: All right, you two, why don't you take a rest and have a glass of beer!

You are both great fighters.

This is the most exciting match I've ever seen. Cheers!

They toasted the King and drank the beer. In the second match, they showed even greater skill and the duel became even more exciting. The King thought that Laertes might not be able to kill Hamlet. He prepared two glasses of beer, the one intended for Hamlet had poison in it.

KC: All right, you two, why don't you take a rest again and have another glass of beer!

I was impressed by your skills.

Let's drink a toast to your great fighting spirit. Cheers!

KH: (*Appearing as a ghost.*)

My son, Hamlet.

H: Oh, it's you again.

KH: Look into the beer.

H: Is something wrong with this beer?

KH: You know, I know a lot about beer.

It smells strange.

H: Smells strange?

(*He smells the beer.*)

KC: What are you doing, Hamlet?

Have a drink.

You must be thirsty.

It won't affect your performance.

H: (*Looking into the beer.*)

KC: Come on!

One beer, or two beers.

It doesn't make any difference.

You are a heavy drinker, aren't you?

Now, have a drink.

H: (*Still looking into the beer.*)

Two beers or not two beers, that is the question.

xxvii. Matsuyama Mirror (*By Kei Ohsuga*)

Translation:

Woman: *"What are you doing here!"*

The Matsuyama Mirror (*Matsuyama Kagami*)

Characters:

L:	Lord
S:	Shosuke
G:	Gondazaemon
W:	Wife
N:	Nun

Long ago, there was a small village called Matsuyama, which had no mirrors. In that village lived a man named Shosuke. He was an extremely devoted son. Although his parents had died 18 years ago, he never neglected visiting their graves – not even a single day.

His feudal lord was moved by such filial piety or "oyakoko" and decided to give Shosuke a gift.

L:	Shosuke, you may raise your head.
S:	Yes, my lord.
L:	I heard that you have been visiting your parents' grave every day for the past 18 years.
	I am very impressed with your filial devotion.
S:	I don't deserve such praise my lord.
	I visit my parents' grave for my own satisfaction, not for the respect of others.

L: It may seem insignificant, but not many people can do that.
I would like to give you something.
What would you like?
Clothes? A rice field? Money?

S: Well, I have a lot of clothes and my father left me enough land.
If I have a lot of money, then I won't be able to work as hard as I should.

L: I see.
I admire your words, but there must be at least one thing that you desire.

S: Yes, there is… but it's impossible.

L: An impossible request?
I would like to help you realize your dream, whatever it may be.

S: You will?

L: Yes, I will. What is it?

S: I want to see my father. Just one more time.

That was an impossible request, but the lord could not say that he could not honor it.

L: Gondazaemon!

G: Yes, my lord.

L: Come here.

       How old was his father when he died?

G: He was 45, if I remember correctly.

L: Shosuke is 43, isn't he?

G: Yes, he is.

L: Does Shosuke look like his father?

G: Yes, he certainly takes after him.

L: Is that so?

The lord commanded Gondazaemon to fetch a luxurious box with a mirror inside. In those days, mirrors were very rare. Each province only had one mirror.

L: Shosuke, please look inside this box.

S: What's this?

       You want me to look inside the box?

       My word, it's my father!

       Why are you in such a small place as this?

       It's me, Shosuke.

       Oh, please don't start crying.

       If you cry, I won't be able to stop crying, either.

       Oh, you look so young.

L: Shosuke, this box is a household treasure, but please accept it as my gift to you.

       I have one condition, however.

Don't ever show this box to anyone else.

Shosuke took the box home. Since he was told not to show it to anyone, he hid it in the barn. He snuck out every day to gaze at it in secret.

He bid farewell to the mirror in the morning and when he returned home in the evening, he said "I'm home!"

His wife became suspicious after a while. One day, she snuck into the barn and peeked inside the box. She had never gazed upon a mirror before and was shocked by what she saw.

W: Oh my goodness. He is keeping a woman in this little box!
How dare you take my husband!
Look at your face.
Look how ugly you are!
Why are you crying?
Stop that!
Get out, get out of this box!

Later that evening, Shosuke came home to find his wife crying.

S: I'm home.

W: ...

S: I'm hungry. What's for dinner?

W: Nothing. Make your own dinner!

S: What happened to you? You seem pale.

W: You are hiding something from me.

S: Am I hiding something?

W: Where did you find that woman?
The woman in the box!

S: Inside the box? Why, that's my father!

W: Don't you dare lie to me!
I looked inside to find a hideous woman inside!

S: That's my father.

W: No!
(*She grabs his collar.*)
You are hiding a woman! One who is ugly with dark skin and a flat nose.

S: Oh, don't grab my collar.
What are you doing?
Let go of me. You are choking me.
(*He slaps her.*)

W: You slapped me! How dare you!

His wife finally bites him.

S: What are you doing? You witch!

W: You creep! Two-timer!

Shosuke and his wife never had even a single quarrel before, but the mirror caused a terrible fight between them.

Just then, the village nun happened to pass by. The nuns in Japan shave their heads bald.

N: Now, stop it! Stop fighting!
You are both adults. Act your age!
So what is it? What?
Sho-san is keeping a woman inside a box?
Sho-san, I'm disappointed in you.

S: It's not a woman! It's my father.
The other day, I paid a visit to our lord and he gave me that box because I miss my parents so much.
I was told not to show the box to anyone, so I have been keeping it a secret.

W: No, no!
I'm sure that there is a woman in there.

N: All right stop fighting.
Let me have a look.
If it is a woman, then I will have a talk with her.

This was the first time the nun had ever looked into a mirror!

N: Ha ha ha!

There's no need to fight, you two.

The woman felt so guilty that she shaved her head and became a nun!

xxviii. Shiba Beach (*By Kei Ohsuga*)

Translation:

Wife: *"Actually, it was not a dream."*

Husband: *"Did you tell me a lie? Gosh!"*

Shiba Beach (*Shibahama*)

Characters:

K: Katsugoro
O: Osaki

There are several different types of rakugo stories. Some stories are based on the comical aspects of life and are called **kokkeibanashi**. Others are considered tragicomic human-interest stories and are known as **ninjobanashi**. The human-interest stories often deal with the relationships between husbands and wives, parents and children, and the lord and his men.

The story "Shiba Beach" is recognized as ninjobanashi. Some consider it to be the work of rakugo master Sanyutei Encho, written sometime during the late 19th century. The story is based on these key words: drunk, wallet, and Shiba Beach. There was a time when impromptu rakugo stories based on three random words provided by the audience were very popular. These "three keyword stories" were known as **sandaibanashi**.

༄༅

*During the Edo period, Shiba was home to a wholesale fish market known as a **zakoba**.*

The main character in the story, Katsugoro, is a fishmonger and a drunk who lives in a small, rundown house.

O: Wake up, dear.
Wake up!
K: Don't yell so loudly.
I'm sleeping peacefully.
O: Get up and go to the fish market.
Now!
K: You want me to go to the market?
O: Yes, you haven't been there for several weeks.
Do you remember what you said last night?
You promised me you'd go to the market today if I allowed you to drink as much as you wanted last night.
K: I did?
Well, it's not a problem going to the market, but…
O: Then hurry up!
K: OK, OK, you don't have to shout.
I'll go.
O: I got everything ready for you.

	New straw sandals, a carrying pole, and a knife.
	Isn't it great?
K:	Not really.
	It's great when I can drink my favorite sake as much as I want and stay in bed till late in the morning.
	If wearing new sandals makes people happy, the owner of the sandal shop must be feeling good all the time.
	All right, all right, I'll go.
	(*Placing the pole on his shoulder.*)
	Oh, it's cold.
	Why do I have to go to work so early on such a cold day? I hate this job.
	(*To himself.*)
	It's strange!
	It's usually brighter by the time I arrive.
	All the markets are closed today.
	Oh, the temple bell is ringing. I see.
	My wife woke me up at the wrong time.
	I hate her. It's too early to be here.
	I want to wash my face at the beach.
	(*He puts down the pole, washes his face, and rinses his mouth. He pats his face.*)
	It's really refreshing.
	(*He begins to smoke.*)

They say the early bird catches the worm.

I hope I can catch something.

There's something with a string moving in the water.

What is it?

Oh, it's a leather wallet.

It's heavy.

(*He looks inside and is surprised. He puts the wallet in his pocket, looks around, and hurries back home.*)

K: (*Knocking on the door.*)

Osaki, open the door!

O: I'm coming.

Don't be so noisy.

It's still very early in the morning.

Our neighbors are still sleeping at this hour.

K: Close the door and lock it!

Make sure no one followed me.

O: What happened?

You look pale.

(*Osaki closes the door and locks it.*)

Did you have a fight with someone again?

K: Give me some water.

I hurried home so fast my mouth is dry.

(*Osaki gives him a cup of water.*)

Thank you.

(*He drinks the water.*)

	I've got a big surprise for you.
	You woke me up too early, didn't you?
O:	I'm sorry.
	I realized it just after you left.
	I tried to run after you, but then I thought there was no way I could catch up to you.
	I'm sorry.
K:	You don't have to apologize.
	I have to thank you. Come closer.
	I'll show you something really nice.
	It was so early that all the markets were still closed.
	So I went to the beach, washed my face, rinsed my mouth, and started smoking my pipe.
	Then I noticed a strange string moving in the water.
	I picked it up and I found this wallet attached to it.
	(*He shows Osaki the wallet.*)
	Look inside.
	There's a lot of money in it.
O:	Is that so?
K:	Yes!
O:	How much?
K:	Why don't you count it?
O:	(*She picks up the wallet.*)
	Oh, it's heavy.
	There's a lot of money in it.

K: One, two, three, four ... ten, twenty, thirty, forty, forty-two ryo!
What shall we do with this?

K: It's mine. I mean, it's ours.
I'm the one who found the wallet floating in the sea.
Everything in the sea belongs to the fishmongers.
Don't you agree?
I'm sure God sent it to me.
With this money, I don't have to work anymore.
And you don't have to ask me to work anymore, either.
I'll buy you the best kimono.
Bring me sake.
I'll drink as much as I want today.

He drank ten bottles of sake and fell asleep.
He went to a public bathhouse in the evening, then brought all his friends home to drink with him.

K: Come in, everyone.
I can't tell you why, but today is the happiest day of my life.
Help yourselves to food and drinks.

They sat in a circle and drank till late at night. Katsugoro fell asleep.

Morning came.

O: (*In a loud voice.*)

Dear, wake up!

K: You scared me.

What's wrong?

Is there a fire?

O: No, there's no fire.

It's time for you to go to the fish market.

K: Fish market?

What are you talking about?

O: I'm talking about the bill for the sake you and your friends drank last night.

K: Pay for it out of that.

O: What do you mean by out of that?

K: You know what I mean.

The stuff from Shiba Beach.

O: Shiba Beach?

I don't get it.

K: Are you still half asleep?

We have the money I found at the beach, right?

O: Money?

Who on earth found money?

K: I did.

O: When?

K: Yesterday morning.

O: You didn't go to the market yesterday.

K: What are you talking about?

       I got up early in the morning and …

O: And you started drinking.

       Then you went to the bathhouse and came back with your friends and drank again with them.

       And you fell into a deep sleep.

       I don't know why, but you looked very happy yesterday.

K: Well …

O: You had a bad dream, didn't you?

K: A dream? It can't be a dream.

       It is too clear to be a dream.

       I'm sure I found the wallet.

O: Then, where's the wallet?

       Our house is very small.

       You can easily find it.

       Where is it?

       Oh, dear, pull yourself together.

       You are always thinking about money, so you had a dream about it.

K: I didn't go to Shiba Beach?

       I only dreamed that I found the wallet?

       But I really threw a party.

O: That's right.

K: Don't be silly.

O: I'm serious.

It is your dream that is silly.

K: It was all a dream?

O: Yes, it was a dream.

A dream.

You had a bad dream!

K: Oh, my!

You must be right.

I've had very clear dreams since I was a child.

My mother used to tell me to be careful about those dreams.

O: See?

What are you going to do about this bill?

K: It must have cost a lot of money.

I don't know what I should do.

Perhaps we should kill ourselves.

O: What are you saying?

If you are not afraid of death, you can do anything.

Darling, you should stop drinking.

If you stop drinking and work hard for a month, you can pay that bill.

And if you continue to work hard, it will take only a year to pay down all of our debts.

K: Is that so?

       Then, I'll stop drinking.

O: Yes, you should.

       But can you really do it?

K: I've made up my mind.

       I will not drink and will work hard starting today.

       I'll go to the market now.

       Is everything ready?

O: Yes, I got everything ready for you.

       New straw sandals, a carrying pole, and a knife.

       Isn't it great?

K: I think you said the same thing in my dream.

From that day forward he worked very hard.
And he didn't touch a bit of alcohol.
He went to Shiba every day, so his fish was always fresh.
He was also a very skillful fishmonger.
He soon attracted many clients.
That year, on New Year's Eve ...

K: Osaki, you had your hair done, didn't you?

O: Yes, I had my hair done for the first time in years.

K: You haven't been to the beauty parlor for a long time in order to save money.

       Oh, the house looks much brighter.

	You changed all the tatami straw mats.
O:	Yes, they got dirty so I got new ones.
K:	I see. I like the smell of new tatami mats.

K: We say the newer the tatami mats and the wife, the better.

No, I mean, as for a wife, the older, the better.

O: You don't have to give me a compliment.

K: We have new paper shoji screens, new sandals, a new carrying pole, and a new knife.

You've changed everything for the coming year.

O: It's all because you've worked very hard.

Here, drink this tea.

It's fukucha— lucky tea.

K: Lucky tea.

It's been a long time since I've had it.

(*He drinks the tea.*)

It's tasty.

O: We were having a difficult time several years ago.

K: You're right.

We borrowed so much money from so many stores that we were like walking loans.

You remember when the rice seller came to collect money from us, and I tried to escape, but it was too late?

I knelt down in the corner of the room and pulled the furoshiki cloth over me.

Then he saw the cloth and said, "It's so cold on New Year's Eve that even that cloth is shaking."

I was so embarrassed.

We didn't even have enough clothes to protect us from the cold.

O: Yes, indeed.

By the way, I have something to show you.

K: What are you going to show me?

A new kimono?

You don't have to.

I don't know much about a woman's kimono.

If you like it, I like it, too.

O: It's not a kimono.

Well, I have something to tell you.

Please listen to my story till the end and promise me you will not get angry.

K: Of course. I promise.

I won't get angry no matter what you say.

O: Wait here and I'll get it.

(*She takes out a leather wallet from the drawer.*)

It's this leather wallet.

K: It's dirty.

Is that where you keep your secret money?

O: Look inside.

K: That's a lot of money.

How can you save so much money like this?

You women are really incredible.

O: Why not count it?

K: One, two, three … ten, twenty, thirty, forty, forty-two ryo.

O: Don't you remember this wallet?

K: Well, no …

O: You found this wallet at Shiba Beach three years ago.

K: Now, I remember.

I found it in my dream.

That was an awful dream, but …

(*Looking down at the wallet.*)

O: It wasn't a dream.

It was real.

K: You said it was a dream.

O: I did.

I lied to you.

K: What do you mean you lied to me? How dare you!

(*Grabs Osaki's collar.*)

O: Wait! Please calm down and listen to me.

You promised me you were not going to get angry.

K: OK then, I'll listen to you.

O: I was glad.

I was very glad when you brought the money from Shiba three years ago.

We were so poor, I wanted to keep the money too. But it wasn't ours.

That night, you drank a lot and fell asleep.

I didn't know what to do, and I went out.

Then I met our landlord.

He sensed that there was something strange about me and asked me what had happened.

I didn't want to tell him about the money you picked up at the beach. But he kept questioning me, so I finally told him the truth.

I said everything in the sea should belong to fishmongers, just like you said.

Then he said, "If your husband pickpocketed the money, he'd be put into a jail."

So he took the money to the town magistrate.

And he told me to tell you it was all a dream.

It was a dream, a dream, a dream!

I told you hundreds of times and fortunately, you believed it.

You were so naive.

You changed a lot and started to work hard from then on.

Even on cold winter mornings, you left for work, and you told me to stay home and try not to catch a cold.

I really didn't know what to say to you, and I secretly prayed for you.

Later, the money was returned to me because no one claimed it.

I tried to tell you about it. But I was afraid to tell you because I thought you would go back to drinking again.

You worked hard. And with that money, I paid down all the debts in just one year.

You continued to work hard after that.

And you opened a fish store on the main street this year and hired some young people.

I thought it was about time to tell you the truth.

So I decided to show you the wallet today.

This money is yours.

Please spend it as you like.

I'm very sorry to have kept the truth from you for such a long time.

Please forgive me.

And don't divorce me.

Don't. I love you.

K: (*Pause.*)

I see. What a story! Forgive you? Divorce you?

No way.

I can only thank you.

You were right.

And you are amazing.

If I had spent the money then, we would not have this store now.

Thank you so much for what you've done.

O: Oh, you don't have to thank me.

I thought you'd get angry.

So I've prepared some sake for you.

It's already hot.

I want to drink with you.

K: I thought I smelled something good. It was hot sake.

I see. Can I really have a drink?

O: Of course you can.

I've cooked your favorite food, too.

K: Wonderful!

As I've said, the older the wife, the better.

I'm very glad you remember my favorite dishes for sake.

Thanks.

O: Here you go.

K: Thank you.

I didn't ask you to give me sake.

You told me to drink this, right?

O: Yes, that's right.

(*Katsugoro looks into the cup.*)

K: Hi, how've you been?
It's been a long time since I last saw you.
I'm fine. You, too?
O: Who are you talking to?
K: My friend, sake.
He seems to be happy, too.
It's the first time in three years.
(*As he touches his mouth to the cup.*)
No, I won't drink.
O: Why not?
K: This may become a dream too.

xxix. Short Life (*By Kei Ohsuga*)

Translation:

Wife: *"Here you go!"*

Man: *"Oh, I'll have a long life."*

Short Life (*Tanmei*)

Characters:

H: Hachi
W: His wife
I: Inkyo

H: Hello.
I: Oh, Hachi. How are you?

         Come on in.
H: Thank you.

         Inkyo, did you hear about the Iseya store?
I: No, I didn't.
H: The husband died again.
I: What do you mean, "died again?"

         We die only once.

         We can't die over and over again.
H: The husband was an adopted son. The store owners only had one daughter.

         After her father died, the mother and daughter were left alone to manage the store.

         Later, the daughter got married.

         The couple built their own house near the store.

The daughter's husband was slim, handsome, and good-natured. They got along well.

Later, the mother died, too.

They had a lot of free time because the head clerk, Banto, handled everything that had to do with the store.

Within several months, however, her husband got sick and died.

I: I'm sorry to hear that.

H: It wasn't right for her to be left alone, so Banto decided to let her marry again.

He introduced her to a tall, strong man and they got married.

They got along very well, but after a year or so, he too got sick.

He was bedridden for about two months and died.

I: Oh. I'm sorry about him, too.

H: Next, a stout young guy came and married her.

They were also very close.

They were always together, except when they went to the bathroom.

They ate their meals gazing at each other and touching each other's hand.

And they shared what they ate between them. "Dear, open your mouth, have a slice of my fish."

I was really envious of them.

I: How do you know such intimate details?

H: I watched them when I went to their house to do the gardening.

I: That's in bad taste.

H: Oh, sorry about that.

The current husband got sick, and he died last night.

I: Again?

Now I understand what you meant by "died again."

H: I do not understand why they died so early.

I really feel sorry for her.

Why do you think they died so early?

I: Well, I'm not a fortune teller, so I don't know people's destiny.

By the way, how old is she?

H: Thirty-three, if I remember correctly.

I: Thirty-three.

Hmm, it's considered an unlucky age here in Japan.

H: Unlucky age?

I: Yes, you know, 42 is an unlucky age for men, and 33 for women.

By the way, is she beautiful?

H: Yes, I'm sure she is the most beautiful woman in town.

A graceful beauty!

You would never get tired of looking at her.

	She doesn't look 33. She looks at most 24 or 25.
I:	Is that right?
	Now I understand why her husbands died early.
H:	Do you?
I:	It is the head clerk, Banto, who handles everything that has to do with the store, right?
H:	Yes. He is really hardworking, honest, and faithful.
I:	And they were so close and always together.
H:	Yes, that's right.
I:	When they had meals, they gazed at each other and touched each other's hand.
	They lived together alone in that house, so there was no one around.
H:	That's right.
I:	So, that's the reason.
H:	What?
I:	Don't you understand?
	They were always at home.
	When eating meals, they always touched each other's hands.
	And she is so beautiful.
	They didn't have to work.
	They didn't have much do to.
	That's why the husbands had such short lives.
H:	Short lives?

I: Yes, that's the reason they died early.

H: Why did the men die early if the wife is beautiful?

I: You still don't understand?

H: No.

I: Banto handles everything that has to do with the store.

H: Yes, he is a faithful and hard worker.

I: They didn't go out very often.

They spent a lot of time at home.

H: Yes.

I: When eating, he touched her hand.

There was nobody around.

H: Ah, I see.

He must have been poisoned by touching her hand.

I: Poison?

Why does she have to poison him?

She is not a snake.

Don't you understand what I mean?

They didn't have to work for the store.

Banto did everything.

H: Yes. They had a lot of money, so they didn't have to work at all.

I: They were alone in their own house.

There was nobody around.

H: That's right.

I: She is a graceful beauty!

	You would never get tired of looking at her.
	That's why her husband died early.
H:	Is that right?
I:	You still don't understand?
	They did something we usually do at night during the daytime.
	You know, it's not good to do too much — whatever it is.
H:	You mean, he not only touched his wife's hand, but other places too, like her breast, or ...?
I:	Yes, yes. You don't have to say it directly like that.
	I have been beating around the bush.
H:	I see. Now I understand.
	Why didn't you say that in the beginning?
	You know, I could have guessed it quickly.
I:	Not at all! You are too slow.
H:	(*He leaves Inkyo's house.*)
	Inkyo is really smart.
	I never thought about that.
	My wife didn't understand why they died so early, either.
	They didn't have to work, and they just stayed home and enjoyed three meals a day.
	When eating, they touched their wife's hand and ...
	No wonder their lives were so short.

(*Arriving at home.*)

I'm home!

W: Where have you been?

You have to go to the Iseya funeral.

H: I know. I'm going now.

W: I feel sorry for her.

This is the third time.

H: I'm hungry.

Can you give me a bowl of rice?

W: There's some rice in the jar.

So help yourself.

H: Can you come here?

W: I'm busy doing the dishes.

H: You can do it later.

Come here anyway.

W: What do you want from me?

H: Just come here, and bring me a bowl of rice.

W: As I said, I'm busy right now.

Help yourself.

H: Don't be so cold.

We are husband and wife.

W: What happened to you today?

You are acting so strangely.

H: Don't say you're busy.

Bring me a bowl of rice.

	It's an easy request, isn't it?
W:	All right. All right if you insist.
	(*She fills the rice bowl using her hand.*)
	Here you go.
H:	Oh, god. You didn't use the rice paddle.
	Please use it.
W:	OK. OK, if you insist.
	(*She pushes the rice into the bowl with the rice paddle.*)
H:	Hey, don't push the rice like that.
W:	I have to do this because you eat a lot.
	I don't want to give you another helping.
	Here you go.
	(*She throws the bowl at him.*)
H:	Hey, don't throw the bowl at me.
	I barely caught it! Nobody else could.
	(*Returning the bowl.*)
	Can you hand it to me?
W:	What's the matter with you?
	What is the point of handing it to you?
I:	Please do as I say.
	I'm asking you.
W:	OK. OK, here's your rice bowl.
	Take it.
I:	Yes, thank you.
	You hand me the bowl and I receive it like this.

	Your hand is touching my hand. Heh, heh, heh.
W:	What are you laughing at?
	You are acting so weird.
	My hand is touching yours and so what?
H:	Don't rush.
	Now my hand is touching yours.
	A graceful beauty is right in front of me!
	You would never get tired of looking at her.
	(*Looking at her.*)
	Oh god, I am going to have a long life!

xxx. The Wallet (*By Kei Ohsuga*)

Translation:

Husband: *"What is it that you left behind?"*

Shinkichi: *"A wallet."*

Wife: *"He is so naive."*

The Wallet (*Kami-ire*)

Characters:

H: Husband
W: Wife
S: Shinkichi

W: Did you read my letter?
S: Yes.
W: So it's all right?
S: I got the letter, so I came over.
W: Good. As I said, he won't be home tonight.
S: Where did he go?
W: Who cares?
          What matters is that he won't be home tonight.
          I never get to spend time with you, Shin-san.
          But tonight, it's different.
          You can stay here all night. We'll have fun together.
S: Well, that's what I wanted to talk to you about.
W: Talk to me about what?
          You want to try something new?
S: No, I didn't mean that.
          Well, I just don't think it's good for us to be doing this.
W: I'm not doing this because it's good.

	Quite the opposite.
	I guess I just can't help myself.
S:	Yes, but…
	What happens if someone finds out and they tell someone else and it gets back to your husband?
	Someday he is going to find out.
W:	What's the matter with you?
	I don't understand.
	Why would he find out?
	You won't tell him, will you?
	I certainly won't.
	An affair is not something to brag about.
	If we both keep our mouths shut, how will he know?
	What he doesn't know, can't hurt him!
	Besides, he has his own fun.
	I know he does.
	Why should men be allowed to enjoy themselves when women can't?
	I won't accept it.
	So, what's wrong?
	I'm not saying that I want to run away with you.
	If you meet someone else, I won't stand in your way.
	If she's a good girl, I'll let her have you.
	You don't have to worry.
	I'll be all right.

	It's all right if he doesn't know.
S:	I think it's because he doesn't know…that it's not all right.
W:	Why?
S:	I feel as though I'm deceiving him.
W:	Well, you are deceiving him.
	Then what about me?
	You care about my husband, but what about me?
	He favors you and helps you out all of the time.
	Do you know why?
	Because I'm always telling him, "Shin-san is a nice man. You can ask Shin-san for anything, anything at all."
	You don't have to worry about that.
S:	Yes, but still, your husband…
W:	Oh, I see.
	You don't have to say anything more.
	I'm getting old.
	You're tired of me.
	Why didn't you just say so?
	Fine!
	I understand.
	Well, you don't seem to know anything about women.
	I'll tell my husband everything about us.
	I said I wouldn't, but you forced me to.

(*Pause.*)

Just kidding!

Did you really think I would say something like that?

I was only joking.

I don't want to hear another word.

Let's have a drink.

We'll feel better.

No more of this silly talk.

Come here, Shin-san.

Come close. Closer.

(*Knock on the door.*)

H: Hey, are you asleep yet?

It's me.

W: Oh, my god! It's my husband.

S: What! But, but…

W: All right. Don't panic. Settle down.

Pick up your shoes and go out the back door!

(*Shinkichi dashes out of the house.*)

S: (*Gasping.*) What a surprise!

Good thing she sent me out the back way.

That was close.

I would have run into him.

And me in my underpants.

I knew this was going to happen.

I told her it would. I told her!

(*Checking his person to make sure he had everything.*)

I've got my sandals, the right clothes, tobacco box, and wallet.

Oh, no!

I left my wallet back there.

I left it by the futon.

The wallet her husband gave me!

And the letter is still in it.

The one inviting me to come over.

What should I do?

Leave Japan?

But that would be a waste if he does not read the letter.

I'll check things out tomorrow.

If he says, "You bastard," then I'll say, "I'm sorry," and I'll run away.

Anyway, I should go home and sleep now.

He had bad dreams that night, woke up early, wandered around the town and went to the woman's house.

S: (*In a low voice, scared.*)
Good morning.

H: Oh, it's you Shinkichi.
Good morning!
You turned up very early today.

I didn't know you were such an early riser.

They say, "The early bird catches the worm."

So it's a good thing.

What are you doing out there?

Come in. Come on in.

Honey, Shinkichi is here.

Make some tea for him.

Sit down and have some tea, Shinkichi.

Oh, you don't look well this morning.

Did something happen?

S: Did something happen?
H: I'm asking you.

Let me guess.

You don't drink much, so it can't be alcohol.

Is it gambling?

I don't think so.

Did you have a fight with someone? Not likely.

The only thing left is your love life. Woman trouble?

You are good looking.

What happened? Tell me.

S: You don't mind?
H: How would I know if I didn't hear the story yet?

Do you have a problem with some woman?
S: Yes.
H: What kind of woman?

A geisha girl who refuses to fall in love with you?
Is she a nice girl?
If that's the case, I'll be the go-between.
One thing you must keep in mind is, stay away from married women!
You'll just get hurt.
What?
Is she married?
That's not good.
So what happened?
Are you in trouble now?

S: Well, this man has been very good to me.
His wife is good to me, too.

H: It happens all the time.
When did it start?

S: Last year.
One day when it was raining. Late afternoon.
Then the next day and the next….

H: And how did the trouble start?

S: Her husband was away, so she said I could stay overnight.
I said I didn't want to, but she said this and that,
and I said this and that,
and this lead to that,
and that lead to this….

H:	I don't understand what you are talking about.
S:	Neither do I.
	Then, right in the middle, her husband came home!
H:	What?
	And did he see you?
S:	Did he?
H:	What do you mean by, "Did he?"
S:	I went out the back way.
H:	Good.
S:	No, I left the wallet you gave me.
	With her letter in it saying he'd be away overnight.
H:	How stupid you are.
	You have to tear up that kind of letter after you've read it.
	It's not a good-luck charm, you know.
	So did he read the letter?
S:	Did he?
H:	There you go again.
	I'm asking you!
S:	I couldn't sleep last night wondering if he had or not.
H:	Well, well, there's no hope for you.
	Oh, honey, are you there?
	Did you overhear Shinkichi's story?
	What do you think he should do?
	Any advice?

W: Shin-san, I heard the whole thing.

You're such a child.

If she's the kind of woman that wants to fool around with a young man like you when her husband's away, she is NOT SO STUPID.

If I were that woman, I would send the man out the back way, wait to open the front door, and take a look around.

If I found a wallet with a letter in it, I would hide it. Then I would give it back to you later.

You don't have to worry.

Don't you think so, darling?

H: Oh, yes, yes!

You're right.

Even if he read the letter, a man who would lose his wife to a fool like Shinkichi, would be TOO STUPID to understand it.

LIST OF PHOTOS AND ILLUSTRATIONS

i. Gonsuke's Lantern (*By Kei Ohsuga*) ix
ii. Tachibanaya Bunzo III (*Photo by Kanariya Eiraku*) 2
iii. Yanagiya Koman III (*Photo by Yomuiri Newspaper/Aflo Images*) 12
iv. Kawayanagi Senryu (*Photo by Mainichi Newspapers/Aflo Images*) 18
v. Tatekawa Rakucho (*Photo by Yomiuri Newspaper/Aflo Images*) 25
vi. Sanyutei Kyuto (*Photo by Yomiuri Newspaper/Aflo Images*) 32
vii. Hayashiya Shozo IX (*Photo by Nippon News / Alamy Stock Photo*) 42
viii. Hayashiya Sanpei II (*Photo by Nippon News / Alamy Stock Photo*) ... 46
ix. Yanagiya Karoku (*Photo by Yomiuri Newspaper/Aflo Images*) 51
x. Sanyutei Oraku (*Photo by Yomiuri Newspaper/Aflo Images*) 58
xi. Hayashiya Kikuzo II (*Photo by Yomiuri Newspaper/Aflo Images*) 63
xii. Nankin Tamasudare performance (*Photo courtesy of Kanariya Eiraku*) 67
xiii. Katsura Yonedanji V (*Photo by Ogiyoshisan - Own work, CC BY-SA 4.0, https://commons.wikimedia.org/w/index.php?curid=35727284*) 69
xiv. Katsura Shuncho III (*Photo by Yomiuri Newspaper/Aflo Images*) 78
xv. Tatekawa Shinosuke (*Photo by Yomiuri Newspaper/Aflo Images*) 84
xvi. Shunputei Shota (*Photo by Yomiuri Newspaper/Aflo Images*) 91
xvii. Yanagiya Kyotaro (*Photo by Yomiuri Newspaper/Aflo Images*) 96
xviii. Olympic Torchbearer Katsura Bunshi V, Tokyo, 2020. (*Photo by Kazuki Oishi, Sipa USA/ Alamy Stock Photo*) 102
xix. Katsura Fukuryu (*Photo by Kaya Ogata*) 110
xx. Katsura Utzao (*Photo courtesy of Katsura Utazo*) 125
xxi. Kanariya Koraku (*Photo by Kanariya Kichiyu*) 146
xxii. Kanariya Simon (*Photo by Kanariya Kichiyu*) 156
xxiii. Kanariya Usagi (*Photo by Kanariya Kichiyu*) 167
xxiv. Big Sale (*By Kei Ohsuga*) 181
xxv. Bloodline Stamp (*By Kei Ohsuga*) 193
xxvi. Complimenting a Child (*By Kei Ohsuga*) 200

xxvii. Matsuyama Mirror *(By Kei Ohsuga)* 219
xxviii. Shiba Beach *(By Kei Ohsuga)* 227
xxix. Short Life *(By Kei Ohsuga)* 245
xxx. The Wallet *(By Kei Ohsuga)* 255

WORKS CITED

"2017年2月25日（土）深夜1：45〜2：40: ザ・ドキュメント: 関西テレビ放送 カンテレ." ザ・ドキュメント," 2017. https://www.ktv.jp/document/170225.html.

"新たなるスタイルで落語に新風を吹き込む柳家花緑に その手法や舞台で披露する'新作落語'について、そして巨星・立川談志への思いを聞いた！- インタビュー＆レポート: ぴあ関西版." 新たなるスタイルで落語に新風を吹き込む柳家花緑に その手法や舞台で披露する"新作落語"について、そして巨星・立川談志への思いを聞いた！- インタビュー＆レポート | ぴあ関西版WEB," January 18, 2012. http://kansai.pia.co.jp/interview/stage/2012-01/120118-e006.html.

"橘家文蔵 (3代目)." Wikipedia. Wikimedia Foundation, July 3, 2021. https://ja.wikipedia.org/wiki/%E6%A9%98%E5%AE%B6%E6%96%87%E8%94%B5_(3%E4%BB%A3%E7%9B%AE).

"読書の時間 (Reading Time)." Wikipedia. Wikimedia Foundation, June 28, 2015. https://ja.wikipedia.org/wiki/%E8%AA%AD%E6%9B%B8%E3%81%AE%E6%99%82%E9%96%93.

"劇団四季から落語家に…三遊亭究斗「ミュージカル落語」で伝えたいこと." 大手小町 (Otekomachi). 大手小町, April 22, 2020. https://otekomachi.yomiuri.co.jp/lifestyle/20200227-OKT8T204304/.

"Gidayu-Bushi: Music of the Japanese Puppet Theatre." prezi.com. Accessed September 7, 2021. https://prezi.com/rkg_i7vpbmg_/gidayu-bushi-music-of-the-japanese-puppet-theatre/#:~:text=What%20is%20it%3F,the%20audience%20and%20evoking%20emotion.

"ゴルフ夜明け前." Wikipedia. Wikimedia Foundation, July 28, 2021. https://ja.wikipedia.org/wiki/%E3%82%B4%E3%83%AB%E3%83%95%E5%A4%9C%E6%98%8E%E3%81%91%E5%89%8D.

"Hayashiya Kikuzo Profile (Kouen Plus)." 講演会・セミナー・イベントの講師紹介はコーエンプラス. Accessed September 12, 2021. https://kouenplus.com/profile/hayashiya_kikuzo/.

"林家木久蔵 (2代目)." Wikipedia. Wikimedia Foundation, July 4, 2021. https://ja.wikipedia.org/wiki/%E6%9E%97%E5%AE%B6%E6%9C%A8%E4%B9%85%E8%94%B5_(2%E4%BB%A3%E7%9B%AE).

"林家小染 (4代目)." Wikipedia. Wikimedia Foundation, August 22, 2020. https://ja.wikipedia.org/wiki/%E6%9E%97%E5%AE%B6%E5%B0%8F%E6%9F%93_(4%E4%BB%A3%E7%9B%AE).

"林家三平 (2代目)." Wikipedia. Wikimedia Foundation, August 9, 2021. https://ja.wikipedia.org/wiki/%E6%9E%97%E5%AE%B6%E4%B8%89%E5%B9%B3_(2%E4%BB%A3%E7%9B%AE).

"林家 三平｜一般社団法人 落語協会." 一般社団法人 落語協会. Accessed August 26, 2021. https://rakugo-kyokai.jp/variety-entertainer/member_detail.php?uid=151.

"林家正蔵 (9代目)." Wikipedia. Wikimedia Foundation, August 12, 2021. https://ja.wikipedia.org/wiki/%E6%9E%97%E5%AE%B6%E6%AD%A3%E8%94%B5_(9%E4%BB%A3%E7%9B%AE).

"「ひめゆり」を落語に 桂春蝶さん「命考える機会に」." 琉球新報デジタル. Ryukyu Shimpo. Accessed September 23, 2021. https://ryukyushimpo.jp/news/entry-505092.html.

"Jugemu." Wikipedia. Wikimedia Foundation, September 9, 2021. https://en.wikipedia.org/wiki/Jugemu.

"桂文枝 (6代目)." Wikipedia. Wikimedia Foundation, July 16, 2021. https://ja.wikipedia.org/wiki/%E6%A1%82%E6%96%87%E6%9E%9D_(6%E4%BB%A3%E7%9B%AE).

"Katsura Ryoba." Iampica.com, 2021. https://www.wikifr.wiki/wiki/ja/%E6%A1%82%E3%82%8A%E3%82%87%E3%81%86%E3%81%B0.

"桂りょうば." Wikipedia. Wikimedia Foundation, June 15, 2021. https://ja.wikipedia.org/wiki/%E6%A1%82%E3%82%8A%E3%82%87%E3%81%86%E3%81%B0.

"桂春蝶 (3代目)." Wikipedia. Wikimedia Foundation, August 10, 2021. https://ja.wikipedia.org/wiki/%E6%A1%82%E6%98%A5%E8%9D%B6_(3%E4%BB%A3%E7%9B%AE).

"Katsura Utazo Profile." utazo.web.fc2.com. Accessed August 30, 2021. http://utazo.web.fc2.com/prof/prof.html.

"桂米團治 (5代目)." Wikipedia. Wikimedia Foundation, August 1, 2021. https://ja.wikipedia.org/wiki/%E6%A1%82%E7%B1%B3%E5%9C%98%E6%B2%BB_(5%E4%BB%A3%E7%9B%AE).

"川柳川柳." Wikipedia. Wikimedia Foundation, July 27, 2021. https://ja.wikipedia.org/wiki/%E5%B7%9D%E6%9F%B3%E5%B7%9D%E6%9F%B3.

Kelly, Eliot. "Rakugo Performer Yanagiya Kosanji." Japan Studies Blog, September 11, 2017. https://eliotkelly.com/rakugo-performer-yanagiya-kosanji/.

"禁酒番屋." Wikipedia. Wikimedia Foundation, May 28, 2021. https://ja.wikipedia.org/wiki/%E7%A6%81%E9%85%92%E7%95%AA%E5%B1%8B.

"骨折林家木久扇の代打、息子木久蔵が「笑点」出演 父おなじみの黄色い着物 - お笑い : 日刊スポーツ".(nikkansports.com. 日刊スポーツ, July 4, 2021. https://www.nikkansports.com/entertainment/news/202107040000857.html.

"柳家喬太郎." Wikipedia. Wikimedia Foundation, August 1, 2021. https://ja.wikipedia.org/wiki/%E6%9F%B3%E5%AE%B6%E5%96%AC%E5%A4%AA%E9%83%8E.

"List of Oishinbo Episodes." Wikipedia. Wikimedia Foundation, August 18, 2021. https://en.wikipedia.org/wiki/List_of_Oishinbo_episodes.

"Malagueña Salerosa." Wikipedia. Wikimedia Foundation, July 30, 2021. https://en.wikipedia.org/wiki/Malague%C3%B1a_Salerosa.

"Mito Kômon." IMDb. IMDb.com, August 4, 2010. https://www.imdb.com/title/tt1172114/.

Miyosawa, Yasushi. "Abcラジオ「上方落語をきく会」インタビュー＜桂 りょうば＞（聞き手：三代澤康司."プレスリリース・ニュースリリース配信シェアNo.1) PR TIMES. PR TIMES, February 1, 2021. https://prtimes.jp/main/html/rd/p/000000122.000040629.html.

"Nankin Tamasudare." Wikipedia. Wikimedia Foundation, June 15, 2021. https://en.wikipedia.org/wiki/Nankin_Tamasudare.

"夏と終戦とガーコンと(Natsu to Shūsen to Gākon to)." 夏と終戦とガーコンと｜【西日本新聞me】. 西日本新聞me, August 19, 2018. https://www.nishinippon.co.jp/item/n/442336.amp.

"Noted Rakugo Storyteller Shofukutei Nikaku Dies at 84." nippon.com, August 22, 2021. https://www.nippon.com/en/news/yjj2021082000926/.

"オフィスらく朝. "プロフィール: 健康落語の立川らく朝." プロフィール｜健康落語の立川らく朝. Accessed September 6, 2021. https://rakuchou.jp/profile/index.html.

"オンライン配信】4/22（水）19:30～第3回文蔵組落語会 ゲスト：立川談春師匠." 三代目 橘家文蔵 Official Website (Third generation Bunzou Tachibanaya Official Website). Accessed August 30, 2021. https://www.bunzou.com/116240.html.

"プロフィール: 桂春蝶 -かつらしゅんちょう- 公式サイト." 桂春蝶 -かつらしゅんちょう- 公式サイト | Just another WordPress site, January 10, 2020. https://shunchou.jp/profile/.

Ohkubo, Kristine, and Kanariya Eiraku. In *Talking about Rakugo: The Japanese Art of Storytelling*, 42–43. Los Angeles, CA, 2021.

"Quotations of the 6th Katsura Bunshi." Words of the Earth. Accessed August 24, 2021. http://earth-words.org/archives/9551.

Radio Cafe, Inc. "アーティストプロフィール (Artist Profile/Yanagiya Koman)." 柳家小満ん | アーティストプロフィール | ラジオデイズ. Accessed September 5, 2021. https://www.radiodays.jp/artist/show/180.

"立川らく朝." Wikipedia. Wikimedia Foundation, May 14, 2021. https://ja.wikipedia.org/wiki/%E7%AB%8B%E5%B7%9D%E3%82%89%E3%81%8F%E6%9C%9D.

"Rakugo." Rakugo | ダイアン吉日 Diane Kichijitsu, 2014. http://www.diane-o.com/rakugo.

"RAKUGO FRANCE Équipe." RAKUGO FRANCE-Équipe, 2021. http://www.rakugo.fr/%C3%A9quipe/.

"落語立川流." Wikipedia. Wikimedia Foundation, October 5, 2021. https://ja.wikipedia.org/wiki/%E8%90%BD%E8%AA%9E%E7%AB%8B%E5%B7%9D%E6%B5%81.

"落語家が話芸を活字で残す理由 柳家小満ん師匠すでに２７巻をネット通販. 産経ニュース" (Sankei News). 産経ニュース, January 26, 2018. https://www.sankei.com/article/20180128-TSP745L7EBM2FIZ4DZFKGFS5EY/.

rehow. "'Let's Meet Shame Now!' the band found in hide (X JAPAN), the 20th anniversary live vol.2 of their debut will be distributed for free on YouTube!'" Japan NEWS, September 25, 2020. https://rehow.net/all/659724/.

"産経ニュース "【鑑賞眼】三K辰文舎落語＆ライブ 噺家たちの二刀流 昭和のにおいがするラインアップ." 産経ニュース. 産経ニュース, April 16, 2016. https://www.sankei.com/article/20160417-QQO4746Y6ZIYHO7YOK43APJBPM/.

"立川らく朝さんの訃報に志らく「師匠より先に逝くやつがあるか」." SANSPO.COM. サンケイスポーツ, May 11, 2021. https://www.sanspo.com/smp/geino/news/20210511/geo21051123230023-s.html.

"サンスポ "橘家文左衛門、襲名披露会見で宣言「文蔵の名前を広めていきたい」." サンスポ. サンスポ, August 29, 2021. https://www.sanspo.com/article/20160907-5E5E62AXOBMV3PKQJNHRZPKIZ4/.

"三遊亭究斗." Wikipedia. Wikimedia Foundation, June 28, 2021. https://ja.wikipedia.org/wiki/%E4%B8%89%E9%81%8A%E4%BA%AD%E7%A9%B6%E6%96%97.

"三遊亭王楽." Wikipedia. Wikimedia Foundation, May 19, 2021. https://ja.wikipedia.org/wiki/%E4%B8%89%E9%81%8A%E4%BA%AD%E7%8E%8B%E6%A5%BD.

"Sanyutei Oraku Official Web Site." sanyuteiouraku.com. Accessed September 12, 2021. https://www.sanyuteiouraku.com/profile.html.

"Shinosuke Tatekawa." Wikipedia. Wikimedia Foundation, July 6, 2021. https://en.wikipedia.org/wiki/Shinosuke_Tatekawa.

Shinozaki, Hiroshi. "New Innovation 'Suit Rakugo' Karoku Yanagiya Tries New Work with a Chair." 朝日新聞デジタル：朝日新聞社のニュースサイト. Asahi Digital, December 22, 2008. http://www.asahi.com/showbiz/stage/rakugo/TKY200812220175.html.

"Special Issue Nippon Kichi/ Bakushō Rakugo-Ka No Kareinaru-Gei No Keishō." Accessed October 24, 2021. https://info.linkclub.or.jp/nl/2008_01_02/hayashiya.pdf.

"春風亭昇太." Wikipedia. Wikimedia Foundation, May 2, 2021. https://ja.wikipedia.org/wiki/%E6%98%A5%E9%A2%A8%E4%BA%AD%E6%98%87%E5%A4%AA.

"春風亭昇太の言葉 - 経営に効く！名言・格言 今日の一言：楽天ブログ." 楽天ブログ, August 15, 2012. https://plaza.rakuten.co.jp/madokita/diary/201208150000/.

"永守重信の言葉 - 経営に効く！名言・格言 今日の一言：楽天ブログ." 楽天ブログ. Accessed August 24, 2021. https://plaza.rakuten.co.jp/madokita/diary/201208130000/.

Suda, Yasunari, "「もの＋こと＋ひと」を取り上げながら、地域や企業のリアル・ムーブメントも熟成発酵させている." スローなコメディにしてくれ, 2017. http://www.slowcomedy.tv/978/2/.

"「ちゃんとした日本語を使いなさい」.橘家文蔵が語る「師匠に教わった大切なこと」." 文春オンライン. 文藝春秋, September 19, 2020. https://bunshun.jp/articles/-/40369?page=1.

"立川志の輔." Wikipedia. Wikimedia Foundation, July 16, 2021. https://ja.wikipedia.org/wiki/%E7%AB%8B%E5%B7%9D%E5%BF%97%E3%81%AE%E8%BC%94.

"平成29年11月号 三遊亭 究斗さん（ミュージカル落語家）." 所沢市ホームページ/ Tokorozawa City. Accessed September 22, 2021. https://www.city.tokorozawa.saitama.jp/tokoronews/koho/tokorokko/2911.html.

Toracchi. "『四代目林家小染."とらっちのアホちゃいまんねんパーデンネンブログ. Ameba, July 21, 2020. https://ameblo.jp/toratchi-1021/entry-12612578412.html.

"川柳つくし." Wikipedia. Wikimedia Foundation, January 28, 2021. https://ja.wikipedia.org/wiki/%E5%B7%9D%E6%9F%B3%E3%81%A4%E3%81%8F%E3%81%97.

"Veteran TV Host Katsura Lauded by Guinness for 45-Year Run." The Japan Times, July 3, 2015. https://www.japantimes.co.jp/culture/2015/07/03/entertainment-news/bunshi-katsura-sets-guinness-record-45-year-run-tv-shows-host/.

Yamada, Riyoko. "ワイドインタビュー問答有用：落語が'再発見'された 桂米團治＝落語家 問答有用／729." 週刊エコノミスト Online, January 28, 2019. https://weekly-economist.mainichi.jp/articles/20190205/se1/00m/020/004000c.

"柳家花緑." Wikipedia. Wikimedia Foundation, August 8, 2021. https://ja.wikipedia.org/wiki/%E6%9F%B3%E5%AE%B6%E8%8A%B1%E7%B7%91.

"柳家 小満ん｜一般社団法人 落語協会." 一般社団法人 落語協会. Accessed September 5, 2021. https://rakugo-kyokai.jp/variety-entertainer/member_detail.php?uid=30.

"柳家小満ん." Wikipedia. Wikimedia Foundation, July 28, 2021. https://ja.wikipedia.org/wiki/%E6%9F%B3%E5%AE%B6%E5%B0%8F%E6%BA%80%E3%82%93.

"Special Lecture: Master Yanagiya Koman III (Rakugoka)." JSA Institute, October 2018. www.jsa-net.or.jp.

"Yoshimoto Company (Katsura Bunshi Biography)." 吉本興業株式会社. Accessed August 17, 2021. http://www.yoshimoto.co.jp/bunshi/biography.html.

Yu, A. C. "Bunshichis Mottoi - Japanese Wiki Corpus." Bunshichis Mottoi - Japanese Wiki Corpus. Accessed September 9, 2021. https://www.japanese-wiki-corpus.org/culture/Bunshichis%20Mottoi.html.

Yui, Masakazu. "落語家・川柳川柳さん死去　90歳　「ガーコン」で異彩放つ(Rakugoka Senryu Kawayanagi Dies 90 Years Old)." 毎日新聞. 毎日新聞, November 19, 2021. https://mainichi.jp/articles/20211119/k00/00m/040/104000c.

Emails:

Kanariya, Eiraku. TACHIBANAYA BUNZO III, May 21, 2021.

Kanariya, Eiraku. Anecdotes: Shinosuke, August 19, 2021.

Kanariya, Eiraku. TATEKAWA SHINOSUKE, August 18, 2021.

Kanariya, Eiraku. Anecdotes: Kyuto, August 19, 2021.

Kanariya, Eiraku. Anecdotes: Shinosuke, August 19, 2021.

Kanariya, Eiraku. YANAGIYA KYOTARO, August 21, 2021.

Kanariya, Eiraku. KATSURA YONEDANJI, August 25, 2021.

Kanariya, Eiraku. SANYUTEI ORAKU, August 26, 2021.

Kanariya, Eiraku. YANAGIYA KOMAN III, September 6, 2021.

Kanariya, Eiraku. KAWAYANAGI SENRYU, September 7, 2021.

Kanariya, Eiraku. TATEKAWA RAKUCHO, September 8, 2021.

Kanariya, Eiraku. KATSURA SHUNCHO III, September 15, 2021.

Interviews:

Stéphane Ferrandez. Email interview with the author, December 1, 2021.

Kanariya, Simon. Email interview with the author, August 31, 2021.

Kanariya, Usagi. Email interview with the author, September 29, 2021.

Katsura, Fukuryu. Email interview with the author, September 24, 2021.

Katsura, Fukuryu, Phone conversation with the author, October 27, 2021.

Katsura, Utazo. Email interview with the author, September 27, 2021.

Kanariya, Koraku. Email interview with the author, October 14, 2021.

ABOUT US

KRISTINE OHKUBO is a Los Angeles-based author whose work emphasizes topics related to Japan and Japanese culture. While growing up in Chicago, she developed a deep love and appreciation for Japanese culture, people, and history. Her extensive travels in Japan have enabled her to gain insight into this fascinating country, which she shares with you through her writings.

Her first book, a travel guide to Japan, was published in 2016. In 2017, she released a historical study of the Pacific War written from the perspective of the Japanese people, both those who were living in Japan and in the United States, when the war broke out. Two years later, she supplemented her earlier releases with the story of an infamous twentieth century geisha, who was both a victim and an aggressor, struggling amidst a strict patriarchal culture and a rapidly changing social system. In 2019, she followed up her 2017 release, *The Sun Will Rise Again*, with a book titled *Sakhalin*. The work examines the far-reaching impact the island changing hands had on its inhabitants and resources, and culminates with the tragic events which took place in August 1945. In 2021, she released a book that was quite a departure from her previous releases. Still focusing on Japan's history and culture, the work introduces readers to rakugo, Japan's 400-year-old art of storytelling. Through a series of anecdotes, biographical information, interviews, and rakugo scripts, the author explains why this traditional art form has endured for many years.

Her most recent book delves deeper into the unique and mysterious world of rakugo. In it, she presents the stories behind the storytellers. In the world of rakugo, sometimes the stories which surround the storytellers entice the public as much as the ones they tell on stage.

As an author, Kristine believes that writing from other cultural perspectives encourages empathy and understanding, and at the same time it broadens our knowledge of the events that have unfolded over the years.

You can find Kristine's work on: *Amazon.com/author/kristineohkubo* as well as other major online book retailers.

KANARIYA EIRAKU is an English rakugo storyteller based in Tokyo. He participated in the Tatekawa-ryu in 1984 to learn about the essence of rakugo from the legendary Tatekawa Danshi. He began offering Japanese rakugo classes in Tokyo in 1991; in 2007, he established his English rakugo classes.

He has translated and performed over sixty classical and contemporary rakugo stories. Since 2007, he has performed in front of enthusiastic audiences in Japan, the United States, the United Kingdom, Denmark, Australia, New Zealand, Georgia, Kazakhstan, and Laos.

Eiraku is one of the founding members of the English Rakugo Association in Tokyo. The organization was established in 2020 with the mission to spread rakugo all over the world.

In 2021, he collaborated with author Kristine Ohkubo on a book titled *Talking About RAKUGO: The Japanese Art of Storytelling*. The work features sixteen classical rakugo scripts which Eiraku translated into English and currently performs on stage.

He also offers English performance classes at universities.

You can learn more about Eiraku by visiting his website: *https://kanariyaeirakuweb.wixsite.com/my-site*.

Talking About Rakugo: The Japanese Art of Storytelling

RAKUGO, the Japanese art of storytelling, evolved as a form of entertainment for ordinary people during the Edo period (1603-1867). Yet, it is not an old, dying art struggling to find relevance in modern society.

It remains an integral form of live entertainment and is becoming more international as the rakugo stage once dominated by Japanese raconteurs now features foreign storytellers. And Japanese performers, both amateur and professional, endeavor to entertain us in English.

Rakugo is fluid not fossilized.

All that is required is a folding fan, a hand towel, and your imagination!

In *Talking About Rakugo*, learn what distinguishes rakugo from Japan's other traditional performing arts, become acquainted with its greatest contributors, enjoy some of rakugo's most popular classical stories, and meet the performers of today.

Rakugo is entertainment for the general public and *Talking About Rakugo* is your easy-to-understand general guide.

Product details

Published: June 8, 2021

Language: English

Paperback: 478 pages

ISBN-10 : 1087944422

ISBN-13 : 978-1087944425

www.ingramcontent.com/pod-product-compliance
Lightning Source LLC
Chambersburg PA
CBHW070534010526
44118CB00012B/1128